D1208577

From the Edge of Extinction

From the Edge of Extinction

The Fight to Save Endangered Species

Darryl Stewart

McCLELLAND AND STEWART

Copyright © 1978 by Darryl Stewart

All rights reserved

The Canadian Publishers
McClelland and Stewart Limited
25 Hollinger Road, Toronto M4B 3G2

Printed and bound in the United States of America

CANADIAN CATALOGUING IN PUBLICATION DATA
Stewart, Darryl, 1936—
  From the edge of extinction
Bibliography: p.
ISBN 0-7710-8300-9
1. Rare animals—North America.   2. Wildlife
conservation—North America.   I. Title.
QL84.S74   591'.04'2097   C78-001244-5

Man's population explosion increasingly
threatens the environments of many
animals with whom he shares the earth. He
traps, shoots, and poisons
indiscriminately. He logs the forests and
drains the wetlands. His pollution of land,
water, and air, and his destruction of
wildlife habitats, endanger scores of
species. By these means he reduces some of
the rarest, most beautiful, most superbly
adapted species of our wildlife heritage to
the brink of extinction.

This book is dedicated to the U.S.
Department of the Interior, Fish and
Wildlife Service; National Audubon
Society; Canadian Wildlife Service; Sierra
Club; International Union for the
Conservation of Nature and Natural
Resources (IUCN) and the World Wildlife
Fund (U.S.), together with other wildlife
organizations and individuals who,
through their endeavours have made the
future of endangered species less tenuous.

CONTENTS

		PAGE
Acknowledgements		8
Introduction Man's Effect on Native Wildlife		9
1	Bison	27
2	Great Egret/Snowy Egret	35
3	Beaver	41
4	Trumpeter Swan	49
5	Musk Ox	57
6	Pronghorn	63
7	Hudsonian Godwit	69
8	Polar Bear	75
9	American Alligator	83
10	Hawaiian Goose (nene)	91
11	Sea Otter	97
12	Brown Pelican	105
13	Florida Manatee	113
14	California Condor	119
15	Eastern Timber Wolf	127
16	Whooping Crane	135
17	San Joaquin Kit Fox	143
18	Aleutian Canada Goose	149
19	Columbian White-tailed Deer/Key Deer	155
20	Peregrine Falcon	163
21	Kirtland's Warbler	171
	Epilogue	179
	Bibliography	187

ACKNOWLEDGEMENTS

The author wishes to express his appreciation to the following for their contribution to the production of this book: Keith M. Schreiner, program manager, endangered species; John Paradiso; Vernon Byrd; Ted Joanen; Dr. Jerome A. Jackson; Ronald Jurek; David Fisher; Lovett E. Williams Jr.; Sanford R. Wilbur; Ralph Bailey; Blair Irvine; Robert C. Belden; John Byelich; Jacob M. Valentine; Ernest Kosaka; Howard Leach; Dr. Raymond L. Linder; James M. Engel; James D. Williams; Dona K. Finnley; Robert W. Hines & Beatrice Boone (Audio Visual); U.S. Department of the Interior, Fish and Wildlife Service; Rod O. Standfield and John Shannon, Ontario Ministry of Natural Resources; Ontario Ministry of Natural Resources Research Library; Royal Ontario Museum Research Library; and the Canadian Wildlife Service Editorial Department. Also, L. Anne Welwood for her usual helpful editorial comments; and to my wife, Patricia, without whose encouragement and assistance this book would not have been possible.

INTRODUCTION
Man's Effect on Native Wildlife

From the northern extremities of Canada and Alaska to the southern tip of Mexico, North America offers a more varied climate and topography than any other land mass except Asia. Across its northern rim lies a wide belt of treeless tundra; at the bottom the climate is tropical and the vegetation extremely lush. The first impressions of the abundant wildlife, fine climate, and natural beauty of the North American continent were recorded almost entirely by explorers who arrived early in the history of this vast land, observed it dispassionately and, after exploiting the natural riches, promptly departed.

Man was probably the last of the large mammals to find its way from Asia to North America by way of the Bering land bridge. A great many species, such as deer, elk (wapiti), moose, and caribou had made the journey long before, as had the bison and the bighorn sheep. Among all North American hoofed animals, in fact, only the pronghorn is truly native to this continent.

The direct effects of man – the ultimate predator – and the mutilation of the surroundings which accompanied his settlement, have proved most harmful to wildlife in general. In the course of man's invasion into the New World, the forests, the rivers, plains,

and prairies, suffered changes more drastic than all those undergone during the centuries since the last glacier. The white man
swept over the continent, attacking almost everything that had
lived in harmony with the environment for eleven to twelve
thousand years. Man represented a new factor of the most
dangerous kind.

In addition to the animals of temperate North America, there
was an array of tropical species which established themselves
along the southern border of the United States and Mexico. Peter
Matthiessen, writing in his book, *Wildlife in America*, says that
these were probably the first mainland species to retreat before the
encroachment of the white man into the New World. It may be
that the southern creatures now thought of as rare vagrants to
North America were in fact once native to this continent and,
together with many other species, have disappeared entirely
without record.

North American wildlife first tasted the impact of the earliest
European fur traders in 1534 when Jacques Cartier's men traded
European goods for furs with Indians in eastern Canada. The first
Canadian land-based fur trade operated out of Port Royal in
1605, and Indians spent more and more time hunting fur-bearing
animals instead of their usual moose for the profit of the French
traders; these species included beaver, pine marten, and lynx.

In colonial times, most laws relating to animals were licences to
kill rather than to preserve. The much-maligned wolf, wrongly,
hated and feared even today in some circles, was slowly being
wiped out by man. As early as 1630, the Massachusetts Bay Company offered a bounty of a penny a pelt, and other colonies shortly followed suit. In 1695 South Carolina passed the Act for
Destroying Beasts of Prey which required Indian hunters to turn
in the skin of a wolf or other predator every year or suffer the
consequence of a severe whipping.

The Hudson's Bay Company was founded in 1670 and its
significance in the early destruction of North American wildlife
has been considerable. A company sale of pelts in November 1743
disposed of 26,750 beavers, as well as 14,730 pine martens, and
1,850 timber wolves; and these were by no means the only victims. A further 127,080 beavers, 30,325 pine martens, and 1,267

timber wolves as well as 12,428 otters and fishers, 110,000 ra-coons and a startling aggregation of 16,512 bears were received in the French port of Rochelle in the same year. People today who have no reasonable expectation of seeing most of these creatures in the wild without considerable effort might well look carefully at these figures.

European fur traders listed the skins in order of value in the early 1800s as follows: beaver, otter, muskrat, pine marten, fox, lynx, fisher, mink, timber wolf, and bison. The most numerically affected as a result of indiscriminate hunting and trapping were the bison and the beaver.

During the 1800s, as the settlers surged westward, orgies of hunting and trapping of practically all animal species occurred, creating a shocking record of wildlife extermination surpassed only by the mindless habitat destruction of the 1900s. Towards the end of the colonial period the wilderness east of the Ap-palachian Mountains was largely gone, and with it much of the great variety of animals that made their home there when the first settlers arrived. Moose, elk, wild turkeys, cougars, bears, wolves, beavers, pine martens, and other creatures were encountered ever more rarely as they retreated before the advance of farmers, hunters and lumbermen. Eventually, many creatures disappeared entirely.

The white man has not lived long in North America, yet he has created a record of extinction of various species and subspecies of native wildlife that is appalling. At least seventy animals that once flourished on this continent are gone, most disappearing in the twentieth century. This alarmingly large roster of animals that have become extinct in North America since 1600 reads as follows: eastern elk *Cervus canadensis canadensis*; the Merriam elk *Cervus merriami*; Queen Charlotte Island caribou *Rangifer tarandus dawsoni*; eastern bison *Bison bison pennsylvanicus*; Badland's bighorn sheep *Ovis canadensis auduboni*; Leaf-nosed bat *Monophyllus frater*; Southern California kit fox *Vulpes macrotis macrotis*; Puerto Rican isolobodon *Isolobodon por-toricensis*; sea mink *Mustela macrodon*; Puerto Rican nesophones *Nesophyontes edithae*; Steller's sea cow *Hydrodamalis stelleri*; Gull Island vole *Microtis nesophilus*; Atlantic Gray whale

Eschricbhtius gibbonus; Great Plains wolf *Canis lupus nubilus;*
Cascade Mountain wolf *C.1. fuscus;* Mogollon Mountain wolf
C.1. mogollonensis; southern Rocky Mountain wolf *C.1. youngi;*
gray Texas wolf *C.1. monstrabilis;* Newfoundland wolf *C.1.
beothucus;* great auk *Pinguinus impennis;* Labrador duck *Camp-
torhynchus labradorium;* Palas cormorant *Phalacroeoax per-
spillatus;* Oahu akepa *Loxops coccinearufa;* Hawaii akialoa
Hemignathus obscurus obscurus; Lanai akialoa *H.o. lanaiensis;*
Oahu akialoa *H.o. lictensteinii;* Lanai alauwahio *Loxops
maculata montana;* greater amakihi *Loxops sagittirostris;* Laysan
apapane *Himatione sanguinea freethii;* grosbeak finch *Psittostra
kona;* heath hen *Tympanuchus cupido cupido;* kioea *Chaetoptila
angustifluma;* greater koafinch *Psittirostra palmeri;* lesser
koafinch *Psittirostra flaviceps;* black mamo *Drepanis funerea;*
Hawaii mano *Drepanis pacifica;* Laysan millerbird *Acrocephalus
familiaris familiaris;* Oahu nukupuu *Hemignathus lucidus
lucidus;* Hawaii oo *Moho nobilis;* Molokai oo *Moho bishopi;*
Oahu oo *Moho apicalis;* Carolina parakeet *Conuropsis carolinensis carolinensis;* Louisiana parakeet *C.c. ludociana;* Mauge's
parakeet *Aratinga choiropteramaugei;* Culebra Puerto Rican par-
rot *Amazona vitata gracilipes;* passenger pigeon *Ectopistes
migratorius;* Laysan rail *Porzanula palmeri;* sandwich rail *Pen-
nula sanwichensis;* Lanai thrush *Phaeornis obscurus lanaiensis;*
Oahu thrush *P.o. oahensis;* ula-ai-hawane *Ciridops anna;* Town-
send's bunting *Spiza townsendi;* Guadalupe petrel *Oceanodroma
macrodactyla;* black-capped petrel *Pterodroma hasitata;* thicktail
chub *Gila crassicauda;* Pahrump Ranch killifish *E.1. pahrump;*
Leon Springs pupfish *Cyprinodon bovinus;* Utah Lake sculpin
Cottus echinatus; Big Spring spinedace *Lepidomeda mollispinis
pratensis;* Pahranagat spinedace *Lepidomeda altivelis;* Ash
Meadows springfish *Empetrichthys merriami;* Raycraft Ranch
springfish *E. latos concavus;* harelip sucker *Lagochila lacera.*

As the world has evolved extinction has been the ultimate fate
of most life forms. Two-thirds of the species of animals and plants
known to have existed are now extinct. Natural extinction is a
slow process: a species evolves over millennia and then, as conditions gradually change, and as new life forms appear, the animal
or plant fails to adjust fully to the new environment and it disap-

pears, equally slowly, to be supplanted by creatures better able to survive. For example, dinosaurs were enormously successful while the world was a much warmer place than it is now, but when the earth's climate became cooler these huge reptiles were gradually replaced by warm-blooded mammals, better able to withstand temperature extremes.

Man-made extinction, however, is quite a different situation; it is final and does not provide new species to replace those that have disappeared.

It was a combination of man, and the introduction of such rapacious mammals as rats and cats, that contributed to the demise of the great auk. This is one of the few creatures whose final hours are known with certainty. Ordinarily, the last members of a species die in solitude, their time of passing from the earth unknown. The great auk was a living creature that died needlessly, one of the first native North American species to become extinct by the hand of man. It was shortly to be followed into oblivion by many other creatures.

The great auk, or garefowl, as it was commonly known, is thought to have nested as far south as the coast of Maine, with a wintering population in Massachusetts Bay, but the southern colonies they formed were probably destroyed quite early. Because it was flightless it was forced to nest on low, accessible ledges in coastal rock areas, and with the invasion of white man its colonies were soon extirpated except for those on remote rocks out at sea. With sticks and paddles meat-hungry mariners bludgeoned thousands of these helpless birds on the bloodstained rocks. The largest great auk colony was probably at Funk Island off the coast of Newfoundland where Jacques Cartier, as early as 1534, salted down five or six barrels of these hapless birds for each ship in his expedition. Early travellers and fishermen visited the auk's nesting grounds each year to slaughter vast numbers for their flesh, feathers, and oil. Rendering the carcasses into cooking oil became an important industry and Funk and other islets became headquarters where auks were boiled in huge trypots, with other specimens serving as fuel. The last great auk was taken on Eldey Island off Iceland in 1844. About seventy stuffed specimens preserved in collections are all that remain of this unique species.

The clearing of the forests for agricultural purposes has been blamed for the extinction of the passenger pigeon, whose most important foods were beechnuts, acorns, and chestnuts. However, most authorities agree that persecution by man was the chief cause of this bird's demise. The passenger pigeon was perhaps the most numerous of all our birds and in its prime was to be counted in billions. Alexander Wilson, the "Father of American Ornithology," estimated that a flock of wild pigeons, seen by him near Frankfort, Kentucky, about 1808, contained at least 2,230,272,000 individuals. John James Audubon, the famed bird artist, wrote that in 1805 he saw schooners at wharfs in New York City loaded in bulk with pigeons caught along the Hudson River, which were sold at one cent each.

The species continued in abundance until about 1860 when, as a result of increasing slaughter for food, it began rapidly to diminish in numbers and no large flock was ever recorded after 1888. When they roosted passenger pigeons were attacked by men armed with guns, poles, clubs, even pots of sulphur, and wagon-loads of birds were killed nightly. Similar methods of destruction were employed when the birds were nesting. At this season the squabs were especially desired, and the trees were shaken or felled to obtain them. When the hunters had taken what they wanted, droves of hogs were released beneath the nesting trees to feed on the remaining birds. At one of the last known large passenger pigeon nesting sites near Petoskey, Michigan in 1878, it is estimated that one billion birds were killed during the season.

Since reproduction success decreased with the decline in numbers and since the pigeons only laid one egg at a time, this species was unable to keep up its reproductive level. Martha, the last member of this species, died in the Cincinnati Zoo in 1914.

The Labrador duck became extinct so early that little is known about it. Its nesting grounds were never discovered, though it was assumed to have bred on the Labrador coast, once the favourite grounds of eider and other sea ducks, pursued for their feathers and down. It is known, however, that this small, pretty, black and white duck flew south in winter at least as far as Chesapeake Bay.

Between 1750 and 1760, a great many "feather voyages" were

made to Labrador from the New England colonies and, though these were abandoned shortly thereafter for the want of available victims, the native Indians and fishermen maintained a steady pressure on the remaining nests and eggs. The Labrador duck never recovered from this early onslaught, and the last specimen was officially reported in 1875, on Long Island Sound, off the coast of New York.

Carolina parakeets had ranged in abundance throughout the southeastern and central United States where their primary habitat was the cypress swamps and woodlands of the deep South. Like the passenger pigeon, they travelled in large flocks. Flying swiftly, they had a piercing cry which must have been quite annoying to the ear of man. Despite the raucousness of their voices they were useful birds. Sheep farmers along the Ohio and Mississippi Rivers favoured them because of their fondness for cockleburs. The farmers wanted the parakeets to devour the burs so that they would not become imbedded in the wool of their sheep and make processing very difficult.

The Carolina parakeet population diminished in proportion to the increases in human population. Destroying unripened oranges, apples and peaches, they were destroyed in turn by outraged fruit growers. Entire flocks were slaughtered when unhurt birds returned to hover screaming over the dead and wounded, making themselves easy targets. In addition, their brilliant, deep green plumage, orange-red heads, with yellow collar feathers, made them popular decorations for ladies' hats in the 1880s and 1890s when vast numbers were slaughtered for the millinery trade. These small parrots were also eagerly bought throughout North America and Europe, as they made intelligent and attractive pets, and were put in cages where they usually died without issue. Only belatedly did their status arouse concern as reports from the wild grew sporadic. On February 21, 1918, the last captive bird died; the species had come to an end.

In every respect the loss of the heath hen, the nominate subspecies of the greater prairie chicken, was a major one. Perhaps the most disheartening aspect of its final disappearance is the fact that prolonged, conscientious efforts to save it had failed.

The heath hen was found from Maine to Virginia, according to

15

early records, where it was believed to have been abundant. It proved excellent dinner fare for the settlers along the eastern seaboard during early colonial days. It was hunted with ease and little thought was given to its preservation. A few regulatory laws were passed, but these were disregarded and the bird began to decline drastically.

In 1890 a search revealed that there were between 120 and 200 heath hens living on Martha's Vineyard, an island off the coast of Massachusetts. However, the effect of poaching and feral cats and dogs continued to carve away at the remaining population.

By 1906 there were just seventy-seven specimens left. By 1908 Boston conservationists could find only sixty specimens and they stringently applied rules governing their safety. The birds' population rose to 300 in 1910, to 1,000 in 1914, and to almost 2,000 in 1916. However, in that year a devastating fire ravaged the scrubby undergrowth of the Atlantic island, aided by offshore winds. The population sharply declined and the area was too small to support the remaining numbers. There was excessive inbreeding and disease and by 1925, only twenty-four heath hens remained. The species was on its way out. In April 1931, the last specimen, a male bird, was carefully captured and banded. It was then seven years old, and as it appeared to be in good health, naturalists still hoped that a mate existed for it somewhere out in the scrub brush but one was not found. On March 11, 1932, the last heath hen was dead.

Not all persecuted wildlife, however, declines inevitably to oblivion. Some, with man's assistance and with luck, escape extinction and once again their populations climb to a level which guarantees continuation of the species.

The last wild bison herd in the United States was down to thirty-nine in Yellowstone National Park by 1900. Yellowstone, founded in 1872 as the first United States national park, had become an ark for wildlife, and was the first of a fleet of arks launched just in time to carry our wildlife through what biologists have called a century of extinction.

Statistics for three months during 1913, as compiled by conservationist Dr. William Hornaday, and published by the New York Zoological Society, were staggering in their enormity. In the

London market alone, sales records for this period included the sale of 41,090 hummingbirds, 10,698 birds of paradise, 13,598 egrets and herons, and 18,936 other birds. Tail plumes from great and snowy egrets native to southern Florida were sold by the ounce under the trade name "aigrettes," each ounce representing six male egrets killed at the beginning of the annual nesting season. The 21,528 ounces of aigrettes sold during the same three-month period meant the death of 129,168 of these birds and the termination of many nests. Such senseless butchery, for so trivial a reason as feather decorations, incensed Dr. Hornaday, whose indignation was shared by members of the Royal Society for the Protection of Wild Birds in Britain and the Audubon Society in America. This conservation awareness led to further laws.

One of the most famous battles waged on behalf of vanishing birds was undertaken just prior to the First World War. For a while it looked as if several species of elegant egrets and herons and about sixty other bird species might end up as the Carolina parakeets did, as victims of the rapacious plume hunters, serving the vanities of ladies of high fashion in New York, London, and Paris. But in 1900 the Lacey Act made the interstate shipment of birds killed in violation of the state laws a federal offence. In addition, the American Ornithologists' Union, together with the newly founded National Association of Audubon Societies, helped end the slaughter of wading birds, terns, and songbirds.

The twentieth century dawned on an era of conservation that saw the creation of national parks and refuges, the emergence of animal protection societies, and the passing of laws to preserve the animals that survived the conquest of the continent. Many species that barely survived the nineteenth century would now flourish under the care of the game manager, a new brand of conservationist primarily employed to provide quarry for hunters and fishermen. The beaver, saved when the silk topper supplanted the fashionable felted beaver hat, was nearly extinct at the turn of the century. The egrets, for which game warden Guy Bradley gave his life, still grace the Florida Everglades.

The sharp focus of state and federal agencies on game species had its foundation around the turn of the century, when freebooting market hunting and habitat destruction had brought

17

catastrophe to much of the continent's wildlife. Bison were nearly gone, as were pronghorn, and a host of other species. Families still lived close to the land and were not many years removed from a dependence on wild game for food and furs. Hunters and fishermen banded together and got state legislatures to pass laws setting closed seasons and hunting limits. Next, hunting and fishing licences were introduced to raise funds for paying wardens to enforce the new game laws. Today every state and province has its wildlife agencies whose primary responsibility it is to ensure the welfare of game species.

The beneficial attitude towards wildlife which flourished at that time did not apply equally to all species. Paradoxically, a certain element of the fauna fell victim as never before to widespread animosity; these were the predatory animals which were branded as vermin, even by many professional zoologists. The birds of prey, or raptorial birds, enjoyed an uneasy sanctuary in some parts of their range, but carnivorous mammals were everywhere persecuted under that "tool" of wildlife management known today as predator control.

The years between 1900 and 1913, which culminated in the Seal Treaty of 1911, the U.S. Federal Tariff Act, and the Weeks-McLean Act, witnessed the first significant federal intervention in the cause of wildlife conservation and the foundation of a United States federal refuge system, which was to reclaim a number of valuable wildlife species from near extinction.

In 1903, President Theodore Roosevelt set aside Pelican Island in Florida as a preserve and breeding ground for native birds. This was the first national wildlife refuge. From this modest beginning seventy-five years ago, the National Wildlife Refuge System has grown into 385 havens totalling 30 million acres and sustaining almost every kind of wildlife species in the United States.

In 1916, the United States and Canada signed the Migratory Bird Convention Act, offering protection for birds that regularly crossed the borders of these two nations. This new international recognition of nature's contempt for political boundaries was enlarged in 1936, when the United States and Mexico signed a similar treaty protecting migratory birds in the southern half of North America.

The history of wildlife exploitation and conservation in Canada has run more or less parallel to that in the United States ever since the first fishery stations and fur-trading posts were established along the St. Lawrence River.

Conservation legislation has run the same course in Canada as it has elsewhere. The Northwest Game Act in 1906 which, as amended in 1917, controlled the taking of fur animals, as one of its protective measures, was a large step forward. Although the wildlife of Canada has been seriously diminished, the country is still in a position to preserve the future representative populations of virtually all its fauna. The conservation movement in Canada commenced, as in the United States, with the establishment of large national parks, and both countries worked together almost from the beginning.

The great auk and the Labrador duck are perhaps the sole North American species to whose demise Canada's contribution has been significant. That Canada has been spared the enormous animal losses of the United States in extinct species is due probably less to superior foresight than to resistance to explore a more formidable wilderness.

The Canadian Pacific Railway, completed in 1885, encouraged the authorization in that year of Banff National Park, the first of its kind in Canada. The magnificent Jasper Park, in the same region, was among the four other parks that had been set up by 1908, and a number of others, both national and provincial, now preserve wild areas of land.

The Waterton Park and Quetico Forest Reserve adjoin and complement Glacier National Park in Montana and the Minnesota National Forest, their respective counterparts in the United States, and there are as well a number of enormous game preserves in the Yukon and Northwest Territories on which hunting and trapping rights are restricted to Eskimos and Indians. The total area of these preserves is more than half a million square miles, or nearly twice the national forest holdings in the United States. Co-operation between Canadian and United States conservation groups has been extensive and effective. The treaties protecting the fur seal and the migratory birds were fine early examples, and the Canadian breeding grounds of the latter are the joint concern of both nations.

Wood Buffalo National Park was established by federal legislation in 1922 in the Northwest Territories and Alberta, originally to preserve the last descendants of the wood bison; it also contains the last known breeding grounds of the whooping crane. Over ten thousand square miles in area, it is several times the size of Yellowstone National Park, the largest park in the United States. This landmark legislation, the first federal law exclusively devoted to the welfare of all endangered wildlife, pledges to conserve and protect, where practical, the various species of native wildlife, including game and non-game birds that are threatened with extinction.

In the mid-sixties much of the continent's wildlife was declining so rapidly that naturalists began to talk in desperate terms. The most recent threat to wildlife and the cause of much of this concern was what has been loosely termed technological fallout. In the course of our efforts to achieve ever higher living standards, production, and income, many new materials and processes have been developed and thrust upon the environment without regard for the consequences that might arise. Perhaps the most serious of those recognized at present are pesticides, but there are a large number of other poisons also in use. We have finally come to accept the fact that some pesticides, at least, have had an extremely serious and far-reaching impact on the natural environment.

Dichloro-Diphenyl-Trichloro-Ethane (DDT) was just the first and best known of the synthetic compounds that seemed the answer to mankind's long war on insect pests. Its application could be modified to suit particular crops, whether wheat, potatoes, cotton, or pulpwood. Initially, this chemical was used in the Second World War. It was dusted inside the clothing of soldiers and civilians as it presumably protected the spread of body lice and fleas that carried dreaded diseases such as typhoid fever and bubonic plague. Later the chemical was sprayed on ponds and marshes where mosquitoes would absorb lethal doses. Thus the poison controlled malaria and spared millions of people from death. In later use DDT was spread by farm vehicles and low-flying planes over fields and forests, wiping out potato beetles, boll weevils, spruce budworm, and other noxious insects. The yield of food was virtually approved by everyone. The Swiss chemist, Paul Muller, who discovered the pesticide properties of this chemical, was granted the Nobel Prize for physiology and medicine in 1948, with unanimous approval.

No one could foresee the far-reaching effects of DDT and the other chlorinated hydrocarbons that were soon to be developed. These chlorinated hydrocarbon pesticides came to be known as the "deadly seven," which apart from DDT, included aldrin, chlordane, dieldrin, endrin, heptachlor, and lindane. However, after a while insect pests acquired an immunity to the poisons, and the survivors showed a tolerance for two or three times the dose that had killed 99 per cent of previous generations, and they were able to reproduce successfully.

By 1962, when Rachel Carson's book *Silent Spring* was published, a few people had already noticed a relationship between elm trees sprayed with DDT to kill bark beetles that create the Dutch elm disease and the death of robins. The indications were clear that the more pesticide-ridden worms a robin ate, the sooner the bird displayed symptoms of twitching and convulsions that culminated in death.

The top predators, especially fish-eating birds of prey, were found to be most vulnerable to this new chemical hazard because they prey mainly on the unwary, the sick, the dying, and the dead, those most heavily laden with pesticide poisons. Each meal adds measurably to the concentration held in their own bodies. Even if they grow to maturity, reproduction suffers in the failure of eggs to provide the usual amount of calcium in the eggshell. The too-thin eggshells, unable to withstand the wear and tear of incubation, fail to hatch. Consequently, raptor populations declined drastically. However, since the almost total ban on the use of DDT in Canada in 1971, and in the United States in 1972, many of these populations have shown signs of a slight resurgence.

Today, most biologists agree that the major threat to animals is destruction of their living space through the expansion of man's growing population. "The primary cause of endangerment to animal and plant forms is environmental destruction," asserts one expert in the U.S. Office of Endangered Species. "Man's ability to destroy habitats has increased manifold over the past half century." In the desperate search for more available land, farmers are encroaching at an ever-increasing rate onto forest lands around the world, forcing the wildlife into ever smaller areas.

In 1966, Senator Karl Mundt of South Dakota introduced a bill on the floor of the Senate to create an Endangered Species Bureau in the Department of the Interior that would "bring threatened species in out of the wild and attempt to raise them in captivity." Mundt prodded and cajoled his colleagues into passing what they laughingly called the "Dickey Bird Bill of 1966." However no one is laughing today for the bill is considered one of the most important pieces of legislation in the long history of man's relationship to his environment.

In that year, the U.S. Endangered Species Conservation Act was formed, giving authority to the Secretary of the Interior to publish a list of native animals that were threatened with extinction. In a world in which life forms are interdependent, endangered species constitute a sensitive barometer of health of the entire ecosystem, and the barometer had reached an all-time low.

Fanatical sponsorship of endangered species for their own sake is not effective in giving these animals the attention they richly deserve. In the past, the people who have given the most support to North American wildlife are the very people who kill animals – hunters and trappers, who contribute a great deal to the financial support of wildlife management. Fortunately, wildlife management philosophies are changing, and in 1973 the U.S. Department of the Interior distributed to the various states $26,500,000 for land acquisition. National wildlife refuges, many of which operated in the past as game reserves, are experimenting with an incentive plan to change management practices. Managers are rewarded for protecting endangered species and hunting guides are learning that some people will pay them for showing how to point a camera instead of a gun at an animal. Several state and provincial game departments are also beginning to care about the preservation of non-game animals.

In 1973, the U.S. Endangered Species Act provided federal jurisdiction over endangered species and made all federal agencies responsible under the act. No less than 109 species and subspecies of native vertebrate animals were listed as endangered. These consisted of seventeen mammals, fifty-three birds, eight reptiles and amphibians and thirty-one fish, plus an additional sixty-nine forms of wildlife designated as "vulnerable" or threatened.

Another important step that has already been taken to protect rare animals is the International Convention on Endangered Species, agreed to by over eighty nations in Washington, D.C., in March 1973. On February 12, 1973, the United States government convened an international conference in Washington for the purpose of controlling and curtailing the international trade in rare and endangered species. Delegates and observers from ninety-two nations attended the three-week-long meeting designed to place restrictions on the trade in threatened animals, halt illegal exploitation, and stop all commercial trade in creatures threatened with imminent extinction. The United States delegation, working night and day, fought hard for a strong, effective treaty, and in the end managed to obtain most of the provisions it wanted.

The Convention on International Trade in Endangered Fauna and Flora, signed in Washington, D.C., on March 3, 1973, included a score of provisions for humane treatment of animals requiring that "any living specimen be so prepared and shipped as to minimize the risk of injury, damage to health, or cruel treatment." The unprecedented language used made the convention, in effect, the first international one. With the passage and signing of the Endangered Species Act of 1973, the United States became the first nation to ratify the agreement.

The World Wildlife Fund (International) is currently launching a drive to convince governments which have not so far acceded to the Convention on International Trade in Endangered Fauna and Flora, which came into force on July 1, 1975, to do so as soon as possible. So far thirty-five countries have become parties. Apart from excessive hunting and the effects of pollution, the convention is considered one of the key methods of stopping the drain on threatened wildlife through commercial activities.

Canada had twenty-three national parks in 1971; today there are thirty-eight. The federal government is to be commended for the recent establishment of three unusually fine national parks: Nahanni National Park, along the South Nahanni River in the Northwest Territories; one on the Cumberland Peninsula of Baffin Island; and Kluane National Park in the Yukon.

The largest wildlife organization in Canada is the Canadian Wildlife Federation, founded in 1962, as the result of the Resources for Tomorrow Conference, held in Montreal in 1961. Its efforts are largely aimed at educating Canadians in the importance of natural resources, especially the necessity of maintaining wildlife species. Although no federal endangered species list has been officially recognized in Canada, a list of ninety-two species and subspecies endangered in Canada has been drawn up by biologists of the Canadian Wildlife Service and the National Museum of Canada.

To date, only in the province of Ontario has there been legislated an official Endangered Species Act (1971) for the protection of provincial wildlife, which at present numbers thirteen species. The province of New Brunswick is currently proposing to initiate an endangered species act, but at this stage it is too early to determine the outcome. The Ontario species currently protected by the Endangered Species Act are: bald eagle *Haliaeetus leucocephalus*; golden eagle *Aquila chrysaetos*; American peregrine falcon *Falco peregrinus anatum*; white pelican *Pelecanus erythrorhynchos*; Eskimo curlew *Numenius borealis*; piping plover *Charadrius melodus*; Kirtland's warbler *Dendroica kirtlandii*; eastern cougar *Felis concolor cougar*; timber rattlesnake *Crotalus horridus horridus*; blue racer *Coluber constrictor foxi*; Lake Erie Island water snake *Natrix sipedon insularum*; West Virginia white butterfly *Pieris virginiensis*; and the small white lady's slipper (orchid) *Cypripedium candidum*. The penalty for molesting or killing a protected species in Ontario is a maximum fine of $3,000, six months in jail, or both. The Canadian Wildlife Act of 1973 provided a firmer base for co-operative studies to protect and preserve endangered species. An example is the acquiring of winter range in the Vaseux Lakes area of British Columbia for the California bighorn sheep *Ovis canadensis californiana*.

In addition, in the United States, millions of acres are managed for wildlife benefit by the states, private groups, and other federal agencies. The U.S. Forest Service has set aside 4,010 acres of land for the endangered Kirtland's warbler in Michigan. The Bureau of Land Management safeguards Nevada's School Spring, home of the warm spring pupfish, and the National Park Service protects the eastern timber wolf on the 540,000-acre Isle Royale in Michigan's north woods.

During the late 1960s the U.S. Department of the Interior, Fish and Wildlife Department initiated a series of "recovery team" programs, which are directed to discovering the biological requirements of endangered species in an effort to reverse the downward trend in their failing populations. This new awareness for the future of nature on this continent is most heartening, especially since the conservation movement is stronger and more developed in the United States and Canada than anywhere else in the world. The 385 refuges scattered throughout the United States play host to eighty-two endangered species, and are the world's largest network of managed wildlife areas. The United States has, in fact, achieved such magnificent results in the field of nature conservation that it is as if this great country is trying wholeheartedly to repair in a few decades what it had destroyed in a few centuries.

Public concern has resulted in the protection of many native species, and North Americans are fortunate that they are able to share their environment with once endangered species. They are doubly fortunate that some of these species have recovered to such high levels that once again they are of economic and recreational value. This initial success in the field of wildlife conservation is encouraging but there remains much to be done, as there are many North American species that still cling tenuously to existence. Recent experience has shown that the fight to save endangered species is no longer the lost cause it was believed to be only a few years ago.

CHAPTER 1

BISON *Bison bison*

When Hernando Cortez, the Spanish conqueror of Mexico, first set eyes on the bison in 1521, he believed it to be rare. According to Peter Matthiessen in *Wildlife in America,* Cortez had never seen anything like it and since the Aztec ruler Montezuma had given it a place of honour in the magnificent square in front of his palace, he had every reason to believe it was the lone survivor of its kind. It was nine years later that another Spaniard, with little claim to fame and apparently no purpose in the New World other than to escape the Spanish authorities, wandered into what is now the State of Texas and discovered the animal in great numbers.

An estimated 60,000,000 bison, commonly called buffalo, roamed much of the North American continent before the coming of the white man. They undoubtedly formed the greatest large mammal congregations that ever existed on earth; huge bison herds moved like a black sea across the plains, covering them for miles around. In 1680, René-Robert Cavalier, Sieur de la Salle, reported that he found the Illinois prairie alive with bison, and though principally animals of the great plains, small herds of these animals were also seen as far east as western New York, Pennsylvania, and in portions of New England, south to the woodlands of Georgia.

To the early French voyageurs, the bison reminded them of the European oxen, and they called them "les boeufs." This name easily became corrupted to "buffle" by the uneducated English-speaking settlers, then "buffelo" and finally "buffalo." True buffaloes, such as the Cape buffalo from South Africa, and the water buffalo of the Far East, or the anoa of Celebes, have horns with ridges, not round in a cross-section. By contrast, the horns of bison are circular, or nearly so.

There are two surviving subspecies of bison native to North America: the plains bison *Bison bison bison*, the typical form that roamed the prairies in vast numbers; and the wood bison *Bison bison athabascae* of the Canadian woodlands, larger and darker than the plains bison with longer, thinner, horns. This race, which formerly ranged from Saskatchewan and Alberta, south to Colorado, is regarded as being more closely allied to the European bison *Bison bonasus* than to the plains bison. The eastern bison *Bison bison pennsylvanicus*, which became extinct about 1850, was a darker coloured animal, almost black, with a much smaller hump.

The bison is North America's largest land animal; bulls of this cattle-like species may weigh up to 2,400 pounds, attain a length of twelve feet and stand six feet at the shoulder. Its massive head and humped shoulders, chin beard, short incurved horns, and dark brown colour, with a mane on the head and front quarters, are recognized by almost everyone.

When the Europeans began their westward drive over the plains of North America, at the beginning of the nineteenth century, the slaughter of the bison began. The last bison seen east of the Appalachian Mountains was a bull killed at Buffalo Cross Roads near Lewisburg, Pennsylvania in 1801; the last seen east of the Mississippi River were a cow and her calf, shot at Valley Head, West Virginia, in 1825.

However, an estimated 40,000,000 bison still survived in the West as late as 1830, and it was not until the construction of the Central Pacific and Union Pacific Railroads in 1869 that the herds began to be annihilated. The animals' last days began in the 1870s, but even then they seemed to march without end. Near Fort Hays, Kansas, in September of 1871, a troop of the Sixth Cavalry came upon a herd that numbered in the hundreds of thousands. "For six days," reported the young commander, "we continued our way through this enormous herd, during the last three of which it was

29

in constant motion across our path." He found it "impossible to approximate the millions."

Some of the killing was for meat or hides but much of it was for sport. In many instances, even when bison were killed for food, only the tongue was saved, and it is estimated that the ignorance in methods of curing hides resulted in the saving of only one out of every three or four hides. In the late 1800s, professional bison hunters, such as William F. Cody, better known as "Buffalo Bill," were hired to supply food for their crews. "I killed buffalo for the railroad company for twelve months, and during that time the number I brought into camp was kept account of and at the end of that period I had killed 4,280 buffalo." Between 1872 and 1874 well over a million animals were shot yearly. No population could withstand such an onslaught.

The art of buffalo hunting consisted of shooting the animals down one by one, dropping each animal where it stood, so that there was no fast clatter of hooves to stampede the others. It was a technique learned from the plains Indians, who hunted bison in the same way, but less efficiently, with their bows and arrows.

Many deplored this wanton destruction, but any measure to stop or regulate the carnage was strongly opposed by politicians, who saw in the destruction of the bison a way to get rid of the Indians. The Indians depended almost entirely on the bison, which provided food and rugs for Indians and pioneers alike, and delicacies such as tongue meat for trade in the eastern markets.

The state of Idaho attempted in the 1870s to protect the bison as well as other hoofed animals. A law giving protection to the bison was passed in Congress, but President Grant never signed it and the massacres continued.

By 1889, just eighteen years after Second Lieutenant George S. Anderson saw that large herd in Kansas, there were only 541 wild bison left, mostly confined to the new national park, Yellowstone, in Wyoming. By 1891 there were only 300 and by 1900, only thirty-nine remained. At Yellowstone conservationists had made a concerted effort on the animals' behalf, arranging for the army to protect the remnant herds. The northern herd was simultaneously reduced.

In Canada, as early as 1820, bison had become scarce near Winnipeg, and bison herds last roamed Manitoba about 1861. About 1850, according to Anne Innis Dagg in *Canadian Wildlife and Man*, Assiniboine Indians were starving because of the shortage of bison at Rocky Mountain House, and in 1858 these animals were scarce in the Crow's Nest areas.

In 1883, Indian tribes worked towards their own destruction when they joined forces with the buffalo hunters to trail the remnants of the northern bison herds to the Cannonball River of North Dakota. There, by cutting off access to water, the hunters accomplished the destruction of the entire herd. In that year, the last important herd, comprising about 10,000 animals, was destroyed. Except for a few stray individuals, the buffalo had disappeared from North America.

Peter Matthiessen, in *Wildlife in America*, informs us that the Indians, contrary to popular legend, had themselves been wasteful of the bison. Whenever possible they took the heifers and cows because their meat was much more tender and the hides, being of lighter weight, were more pliable. If their winter store of dried meat was sufficient, they frequently killed the bison for the tongues alone, leaving the carcasses for the scavengers. It was said that a single Indian might consume fifteen to twenty pounds of his favourite cuts during a long night's feast.

Nevertheless, because the Indian population was relatively small, their impact on the bison populations was not of great significance.

It was the white man who, in addition to shooting the bison down indiscriminately from passing trains and other vantage points, had nearly wiped out a species that until its very last decade still numbered in the millions.

In 1905, the concern of William T. Hornaday, the foremost conservationist of his day, and others, led to the establishment of the American Bison Society, to promote the breeding of bison and their preservation in parks and refuges.

Canada entered early in the campaign to save the bison, and supplemented her own wild bands with the purchase of Montana bison in 1909. The plains bison might have disappeared from Canada had not an Indian by the name of Walking Coyote saved four bison calves from slaughter in 1873, during a hunting expedition along the Milk River in northeastern Montana. Also, a Winnipeg fur dealer saved another five calves a year later. The Indian drove his four calves into Montana where by 1914 their descendants numbered 745. In that year those 745 bison and another eighty-seven, offspring of the five calves saved by the fur dealer, were released in Wainwright Buffalo National Park in Alberta. By 1954, the offspring of the original nine calves numbered 40,000, making the comeback of the plains bison one of Canada's great conservation victories.

Wood Buffalo National Park, established in 1922 in the Northwest Territories and Alberta, contains the last descendants of the darker and larger wood bison, a subspecies long since extirpated from the eastern United States. This 10,500 square mile area was created essentially for the protection of the wood bison, which at that time numbered around 15,000. In 1924, in order to save some of the plains bison from an annual harvest (which had been in operation since their resurgence), 1,634 of these prairie animals were introduced into Wood Buffalo National Park. Here, they hybridized with the pure wood bison strain, thus eliminating most of the larger woodland race.

Fortunately, a small herd of 200 pure wood bison was discovered in the northwestern part of Wood Buffalo National Park where they were isolated by swamps, but by 1965 only about 100 remained. In 1963, eighteen wood bison were relocated to Fort Providence, north of the Mackenzie River, to establish an independent herd where two years later they had increased to twenty-four animals. In 1965, fifty-three wood bison were captured and transported to Elk Island National Park in the aspen forest of Alberta.

In the United States, the original thirty-nine plains bison from Yellowstone National Park today number around 800, including privately owned animals. Yellowstone's 800 bison are unique. Only here in the entire United States have wild, free-ranging bison survived since colonial times. In Wyoming the species was first protected in 1890; in 1908 the National Bison Range was established in the Flathead Valley of Montana, to the west of Mission Mountain. There, a bison herd of several hundred animals was developed over the years, some of which have been relocated to a number of reserves in the United States and Canada. A herd has also been established in Alaska. By 1926, there were 4,376 bison left in the United States, while Canada was the home of 11,957.

Today, approximately 30,000 bison exist in North America, where in some places surplus animals are regularly sold for meat or offered as targets to hunters. Bison will never be as abundant as they were when the early settlers encountered them, but breeding and relocation programs have assured the bison's future as part of our natural heritage. The saving of the bison from the edge of oblivion has undoubtedly been one of the finest victories for wildlife conservation on this continent.

CHAPTER 2

GREAT EGRET
Casmerodius albus

SNOWY EGRET
Leucophoyx thula

Imagine, if you will, a small pond in a swamp within the Florida Everglades, with the play of light and shadows reflecting the placidity of a May morning. The sky is alive with the flapping of the large, white wings of innumerable adult egrets, all in nuptial plumage with long filigrees of feathers trailing gracefully from their backs.

The year is somewhere around 1895 and the price of the long, silky breeding plumes is $38 an ounce in New York City. At the edge of the swamp, plume hunters eagerly await the return home of the parent birds from foraging for food for their young. As the birds approach they are shot one by one, stripped of their desirable plumes – and the carcasses left to rot. The young birds vainly awaiting the return of their parents cry piteously in their nests until they succumb to starvation.

The scene was repeated time and time again around the turn of the century. According to wildlife writer Elizabeth C. Mooney, five million birds died annually to satisfy the demands of the millinery trade. Many birds became victims of the plume hunters, from the Arctic tern to the hummingbird, but the great and snowy egrets undoubtedly suffered the most. Record has it that in one

35

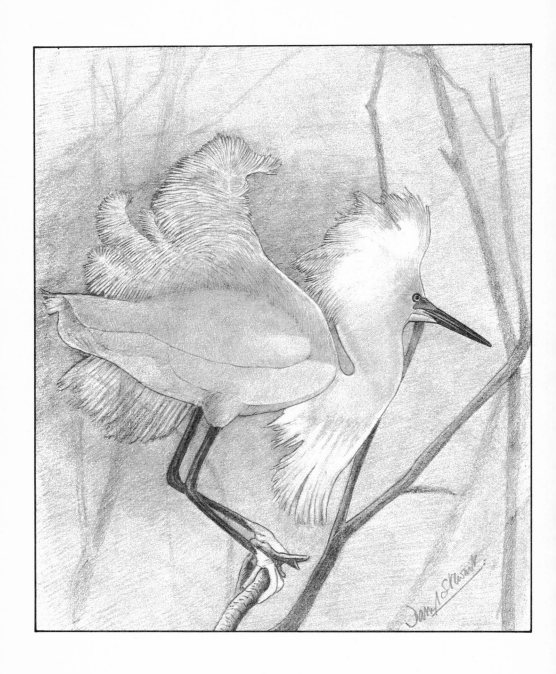

breeding season in Florida, 130,000 egrets were slaughtered to cater to the whims of the fashionable ladies of New York.

Before the feather fad started around 1875, great and snowy egrets were subjected to little other than sport hunting. Then, suddenly, they were recognized as the most accessible and the most lucrative of all species for the millinery trade. The abundant heronries of the Gulf Coast and Florida were invaded by hunters who shot the adult birds and left the young to starve in their nests. Only during the breeding season did the birds carry the graceful nuptial plumes, known in the trade as "aigrettes," which, at the peak of demand, were worth their weight in gold.

"The horrors attending the collection of plumes of Herons is beyond the powers of language to describe, and can best be shown pictorially. The paltry price in money that is paid for the plumes is not to be compared to the price paid in blood and suffering." Thus wrote William Dutcher, President of the National Association of Audubon Societies, around the turn of the century. "Women must remember that the white Herons wear the coveted plumes only during the breeding season, and that the parent birds must be shot in order to obtain the plumes. The young birds in the nest must starve, in consequence of the death of the parents."

The same cruelty was practised in other countries as in North America. Mr. A.H.E. Mattingly of Melbourne graphically described the horrors he witnessed at an egret rookery in New South Wales, Australia, about the same time:

> I could see some large patches of white, either floating in the water, or reclining on the fallen trees in the vicinity of the egret's rookery. As I drew nearer, what a spectacle met my gaze – a sight that made my blood boil with indignation. There, strewn on the floating waterweed, and also on adjacent logs, were at least fifty carcasses of large white and smaller plumed egrets. There were fifty birds ruthlessly destroyed, besides their young (about 200) left to die of starvation. This last fact was betoken by at least seventy carcasses of nestlings, which had become so weak that their legs had refused to support them, and they had fallen from the nests into the water below, and had been miserably drowned; while, in the trees above, the remainder of the parentless young ones could be seen staggering

in the nests, some of them falling with a splash into the water, as their waning strength left them too exhausted to hold up any longer, while others simply stretched out of the nest and so expired. Others, again, were seen trying in vain to attract the attention of passing egrets, which were flying with food in their bills to feed their own young, and it was a pitiful sight indeed to see these starvelings with outstretched necks and gaping bills imploring the passing birds to feed them.

W.E.D. Scott, who chronicled the plume birds' slaughter in Florida, visited a rookery at John's Pass in 1880 and counted over 200 spoonbills, abundant reddish egrets, and myriads of great and snowy egrets. Peter Matthiessen, in *Wildlife in America*, informs us that six years after the spoonbills had vanished from the area, and only a few wary egrets remained, Scott's records for the other rookeries investigated were equally desolate.

The dictates of fashion had created an industry which became worldwide. Within a few years growth of this industry was such that Florida, swiftly followed by Texas, passed a law to protect plume bird eggs and young, but these laws were ignored to the same extent as they were hard to implement. In spite of state and citizen concern, the shooting continued. Women, intent on following the style, continued to grace themselves with the shimmering finery of breeding egrets. Egrets were altogether far too easy to kill and continued to perish in horrendous numbers.

The first to raise his voice against the killing was George Bird Grinnell in 1886. Grinnell was the editor of *Forest and Stream* when he published an editorial suggesting that an organization be formed to protect wild birds and their eggs. Nearly 40,000 people enrolled in that U.S. Audubon Society, but the society died out. In the late 1890s Mrs. Augustus Hemenway of Boston read a witness's account of the horrors of the egret slaughter in Florida, which prompted her to act on their behalf. From a copy of Boston's "Blue Book," she drew up a list of acquaintances in order to urge them to form a society for the protection of birds, especially the victimized egrets. In this way the Massachusetts Audubon Society was born.

The outlook improved for the egrets, in 1896, with the resurrection of the Audubon Societies, and by the turn of the century the

American Ornithologists' Union's Model Law was made operative in five of the United States. This law had been enacted in New York and Pennsylvania, but had been amended or repealed, and bird legislation was as ineffective as it had been before any protective movement had begun.

Subsequently, in 1900, Representative John F. Lacey of Iowa sponsored a law which awarded the federal government control over the importation of foreign birds, and also over interstate traffic in feathers of creatures killed in violation of state laws. This measure created a serious set-back to the millinery trade and was entirely due to the efforts of the American Ornithologists' Union and the Audubon Societies. The Audubon operations on behalf of the "millinery species" were to develop into a complex system of federal, state, and private refuges.

The salvation of the snowy egret was due in no small part to E.A. McIlhenny of the noted tabasco family. Peter Matthiessen, in *Wildlife in America*, informs us that in 1892, McIlhenny set aside his extensive private refuge in the hammocks of Avery Island in Louisiana for this species. The refuge maintained a breeding population of snowy egrets in the grim years before they were restored by protection, and remains a marvellous spectacle to this day.

Meanwhile, Audubon Societies sprang up in state after state until by 1905 thirty-five state Audubon Societies had merged into a national association with enough power to influence public opinion. At least ten states appointed wardens to protect nesting colonies and enforce what laws existed.

Among the four wardens employed by the Audubon Society was Guy Bradley, thirty-five, a guardian of wildlife in the Florida Everglades, who was to become the first human martyr in the egrets' cause. On July 8, 1905, warden Guy Bradley spotted a suspicious looking schooner near Oyster Key, off the tip of the Florida mainland. He set out in his skiff and reached the schooner just as two hunters were loading dead egrets aboard. When Bradley tried to arrest them, the skipper shot him at point blank range and set sail, leaving the warden dead in his drifting boat. His body was not discovered until twenty-four hours later when two curious boys rowed over to investigate the reason for the hovering vultures. Bradley's killer, claiming self-defence, went free.

"Heretofore," cried Audubon President William Dutcher, when he heard the news, "the price has been the life of the birds. Now human blood has been added." The murder of Guy Bradley may have been responsible for turning the tide of public opinion in favour of the egrets. The National Association of Audubon Societies was, shortly thereafter, able to push through a law prohibiting the use of wild bird feathers in New York, the centre of the millinery trade.

New conservation awareness led to further laws. In 1916, the United States and Canada signed the Migratory Bird Convention Act offering protection to birds that regularly crossed the borders of these two nations.

Today, both the great and the snowy egret are flourishing once again; the former has even become a summer wanderer into southern Canada. These birds are dignified, elegant examples of our native wildlife, and a constant reminder of the fact that a species can be saved from almost total annihilation if enough people are concerned enough to take positive action to prevent it.

CHAPTER 3

BEAVER *Castor canadensis*

No other animal has influenced a nation to the extent that the beaver has influenced the development of Canada. Its hunched profile adorned the first Canadian stamp and is still carried on the Canadian nickel.

The beaver is the largest of North American rodents, and the largest in the world except for the South American capybara. At one time, in the Pleistocene period – the era of the mammoths and mastodons – giant beavers were found in North America. Their length including tail was probably about nine feet, and they may have weighed 800 pounds. Present day adult beavers average forty to sixty pounds and a large specimen may be four feet in length.

Beavers are animals of lakes and rivers. One of their best-known habits is the construction of dams across small streams. These dams, made from branches and layers of mud and rocks, serve mainly to provide the animals with a year-round supply of water of a suitable depth. Beavers sometimes build large dwellings in these ponds with underground entrances, for protection against predators. However, not all beavers build "lodges," the name for these dwellings, or even dams; in large river areas they commonly use dens in the banks, making the entrances under water. In areas

where winter temperatures fall below freezing, beaver ponds have to be deep enough for the animals to be able to enter and leave their abodes by swimming beneath the ice.

The beaver colony is very much a family setup. There is only one dominant male, which shows considerable aggressiveness towards the males in other colonies and also to young males in its own colony when they attain breeding age. In fact, the latter are eventually driven out. This usually happens when the young males are approaching two years of age, and their mother – the oldest female of the colony – is making preparations for a new litter of young. Leaving the lodge where they were born, the two-year-old males strike out on their own, searching for mates and new areas suitable for starting colonies. The yearling young remain in the old colony, but both they and their father move out of the main lodge before the new young are born. For several months they live in temporary quarters nearby, leaving the old female and her babies in sole possession of the main lodge. Most of the work of building the dams and lodges is undertaken by the male beavers, but the females also help when they are not occupied with their young.

Many North American mammals have suffered from the effects of the fur trade, though no species, except for the bison, was as greatly affected as the beaver had been by hunting and trapping. Exploited, from the onset, for its rich, dense fur, the beaver started its decline in North America as early as 1638, when the compulsory use of its fur in the manufacture of hats was decreed by King Charles I. Fashionable Europeans demanded felt hats, and the soft beaver fur made the most luxurious felt of all. Because the process of felt making involved large amounts of mercury, many hatters were literally mad, their brains addled by mercury poisoning. Hat styles varied considerably in size and shape; some hats were tall, some squat, and others drooping.

For several decades the demand for beaver fur remained strong as fur trappers spread across the continent, seeking fresh supplies as old ones diminished.

Beaver fur was popular in part because this animal was so widespread and numerous. The former range of the beaver extended over virtually all Alaska and Canada south of the treeline, wherever there were streams or rivers bordered by hardwood trees, and at one time included most of the continental United States and a portion of northern Mexico.

The beaver-hat industry became increasingly important and the pelts themselves were the major fur export of Canada. This predominance lasted for two hundred years and makes the beaver the best example of a fur-bearing animal whose numbers were drastically affected by the exploitation of man. The history of the fur trade is essentially a history of the beaver.

In the early days of the fur trade as many beaver pelts were collected as possible by the indigenous tribes, since furs meant wealth with which the Indians could purchase European goods. There was never any attempt to spare breeding pairs of these animals to provide for the future.

Up to 17,000 beaver pelts a year were taken to be sold in London and Edinburgh, most being used for felt to make beaver hats. A very large adult beaver might yield enough fur for eighteen hats. The thick fur, which the hatters of Europe found so desirable, is actually only the inner half of the beaver's coat. A typical fur-bearer, the beaver also has longer, coarser guard hairs which overlie the inner coat to protect it. Garments made by native peoples from beaver fur and worn with the hair next to the skin were not considered comfortable until these guard hairs had been worn away. Generally speaking, the cooler the climate the richer the fur. Prime beaver pelts are found where the average yearly temperature falls below 35 degrees Fahrenheit. Like other aquatic mammals, the beaver will build up layers of fat as required, thus providing further insulation and an increase in buoyancy: its first line of defence against the cold, however, is its lustrous coat.

Indians were encouraged to kill far more beavers than they required and trade their surplus skins to the white man. One beaver pelt would buy a pound of tobacco, twelve would buy a gun. The high regard in which the beaver was held by the Indians in no way impeded its destruction, and since the animal is in fact rather stupid and defenceless, the progress of civilization was everywhere accompanied by its extirpation.

With the founding of the Hudson's Bay Company in 1670 the

fur trade became the chief business of the colonies, exceeding in importance the earlier commerce in timber and fish.

The "fur countries" were roughly that wilderness of forest and lakes which we refer to today as the Great North Woods. In colonial times that embraced the hardwood and evergreen backwoods of the Northeast as well as the spruce-muskeg of eastern Canada, which stretched north from Quebec and the Great Lakes to Labrador and Hudson Bay; the western limits of the fur countries were then unknown.

With the use of steel traps trapping became more and more effective. By 1812 beavers were scarce everywhere in Canada east of the Rocky Mountains, though they were still plentiful west of that region. However, there too trapping would later reduce their numbers, with about 153,000 pelts being collected annually between 1860 and 1870. Shortly after the turn of the century, because of trapping and settlement, beavers became very scarce in western Canada. Throughout much of the continent the big rodent had become extirpated; many large regions were completely without beaver during most of the first half of this century. And had the French and Italian stylists not shifted their interest to the silk hat, the beaver might have followed the dodo, great auk, Steller's sea cow, and others, to man-made oblivion.

Settlement initially threatened to destroy both the beaver and its habitat, but this did not happen. Marginal lands where wildlife thrived were frequently left alone; it was not economically feasible to trap only a few animals when fur prices were not high. Thus, by 1850, beaver were again increasing in number in Nova Scotia, and they were to do so right across Canada.

Fortunately, the conservation of the beaver in fur management by the regular harvest of surplus animals was developed among Indian trappers of northern Ontario in the early 1930s. The practice was successful and quickly spread right across Canada, with the result that the beaver populations quickly increased. More recently, conservation plans have been put into effect by the Canadian federal and provincial governments, with the co-operation of the trappers, and managers have reintroduced beaver back into areas where they had previously vanished. Progressive legislation and improved traffic laws have contributed largely to the increase in beavers, and quotas have been set whereby extra beavers can be harvested, while enough breeding adults are left to keep each region populated. Beavers have again assumed their role of leadership in the wild fur market. During the 1971-1972 season 390,884 beaver were taken in Canada alone at an average value of $17.80 and a total value of $6,445,201.

Unfortunately, with the resurgence of the beaver population, the problem of nuisance beavers has appeared. Their dams plug culverts, thereby flooding roads, bridges, railroads, and agricultural lands, and they cut down ornamental trees on the edges of towns, cities, golf courses, and parks. As a result, provincial game departments have been forced to maintain regular programs of live-trapping and moving the offending beavers to unstocked areas.

In some areas the problem is not how to protect the beavers, but to harvest enough to prevent overpopulation and starvation due to overconsumption of food supplies. In Ontario beavers have become so plentiful that today they surpass their previous population records. In parts of the province the big rodents have penned up almost every trickle of water, and back to back beaver ponds dot the landscape. Trappers take some 200,000 annually and yet the population still flourishes. No one wishes to see the beaver decline to the level which brought them close to extinction earlier in this century, when the famed conservationist Grey Owl argued the beavers' cause in his popular writings and public appearances. But today, because of its great numbers, the beaver is on a destructive rampage that might cause its own demise. Ironically, the trapper may be the beaver's best friend, in endeavouring to keep the animal's population down to optimum levels.

Despite their destructiveness beavers are natural conservationists. The multitudes of beavers on the headwaters of major streams stabilize stream flow and prevent stream erosion. Also they create trout ponds and improve the habitat for many forms of wildlife such as ducks and woodcock, the great blue heron, and for mammals such as mink and otter. Therefore, they merit careful study and intelligent management. Deprived of the activities of the beaver, forest streams would lose much of their variety and life.

In October 1977, a "Bring Back the Beaver" campaign was launched by conservationists in Britain, where the animal became extinct around the thirteenth century. Britain has called upon French biologist Dr. Bernard Richard to rectify the situation, as there are advantages to having beaver about the place for water conservation and stream-flow stabilization. Dr. Richard will attempt to capture seven pairs of European beaver *Castor fiber* from France, to re-introduce them into Wales or possibly East Anglia, on England's east coast.

CHAPTER 4

TRUMPETER SWAN *Olor buccinator*

When white settlers first explored the new lands in the West they saw numbers of large, white swans. These were trumpeter swans, the largest of all the world's waterfowl. At that time, the trumpeter swan ranged widely in the wetlands of the northern forests and the prairie marshes from the Rocky Mountains to the western shores of Hudson Bay, and from the Arctic Ocean to about 60 degrees latitude, and south to Missouri. Trumpeters are the counterpart of the whooper swans that inhabit the Arctic and near Arctic regions of the Old World.

Great flights of swans were observed by these early settlers on the Atlantic seaboard from Maine to Georgia, of which some were believed to be trumpeters. But as man's conquest of North America advanced, the trumpeter swans retreated north-westward.

The trumpeter swan is sometimes mistaken for the far more numerous whistling swan, but the trumpeter is decidedly larger. Its deep, horn-like call is quite different from the high-pitched "whistle" of the whistling swan. W.E. Banko makes an observation of this fact in his book *The Trumpeter Swan*: "The call has a definite horn-like quality over a wide vocal range and may be

uttered from one to a number of times at widely spaced intervals or in staccato fashion. The trumpeter gives voice perhaps most often in flight, but also commonly while on land or floating on water."

This species was originally common as a migrant in southern Ontario and elsewhere in the area of the Great Lakes, where, according to early literature, it appears to have been seen more regularly than the whistling swan. Thomas McIlwraith, an Ontario ornithologist, stated in 1894 that he had seen two specimens which had been killed at Long Point on Lake Erie. And a painting by the nineteenth-century bird artist William Pope, dated April 6, 1847, was probably based on a locally taken specimen. It is not likely that more recent records from that area have or will be obtained.

Just how many trumpeter swans formerly existed on this continent is not known, but they must have been plentiful. An account from North Carolina in 1709 refers to "great flocks in the winter," and in 1795 Samuel Hearne of the Hudson's Bay Company recorded that the Indians took great numbers of these birds for their feathers as well as for food.

Trumpeter swans remained plentiful until the end of the eighteenth century when the powerful Hudson's Bay Company began to take control of all trade, and swan skins came to be regarded as valuable articles of trade. The famous bird artist John James Audubon selected quills from the trumpeter swan for sketching the feet and claws of small birds, because they were hard yet also elastic.

Large-scale slaughter ensued, and the number of trumpeter swans dwindled rapidly. An indication of the decimation of the swans can readily be seen in the records of the Hudson's Bay Company, in which a total of 17,671 bird skins, largely trumpeter swans, were listed as sold between 1853 and 1877. The population steadily decreased from 1,312 in 1854 to 122 in 1877, and during the next two or three years the traffic in swan skins practically ceased.

The trumpeter swan was nearly gone from northern Canada and from the prairies to Quebec by the 1890s. Edward Howe Forbush in 1912 summed up the history of the trumpeter swan's disappearance as follows:

51

The trumpeter has succumbed to incessant persecution in all parts of its range, and its total extinction is now only a matter of years. . . . The breeding swans of the United States have been extirpated, and the bird is pursued, even in its farthest northern haunts, by the natives, who capture it in summer, when it has moulted its primaries and is unable to fly. . . . The large size of this bird and its conspicuousness have served, as in the case of the whooping crane, to make it a shining mark, and the trumpetings that were once heard over the breadth of a great continent, as the long converging lines drove on from zone to zone, will soon be heard no more. In the ages to come, like the call of the whooping crane, they will be locked in the silence of the past.

Apparently, fewer than 100 adults remained outside Alaska in 1932; a few of them in Alberta, and possibly some in the southern Yukon. "This magnificent bird, the largest of all North American wild fowl, belongs to a vanishing race," wrote Arthur Cleveland Bent of the trumpeter swan in 1925. Mr. Banko states that "the effect of such exploitation in the far-flung breeding populations of this species for more than a hundred and twenty-five years must have been devastating and largely responsible for its extermination over vast regions, particularly in the heart of its Canadian breeding range."

The species was thought to have nested for the last time in British Columbia in the 1840s until a flock was identified at Vaseux Lake in the Okanagan Valley in 1922. The area was subsequently made into a migratory bird sanctuary. Unfortunately, the Vaseux Lake population died out as a result of lead poisoning after the swans ingested shotgun pellets in shallow water on the shore of nearby Lake Okanagan. However, other British Columbia wintering spots have been successfully managed, and so have a few wild breeding areas, such as the marshes around Grande Prairie in Alberta.

The Migratory Bird Convention Act of 1916 started the protection that resulted in a comeback for these birds. The treaty put a closed season on swans (and other migratory birds) in Canada and in the United States and later in Mexico.

Because of growing concern for the future of the swan, lectures and advertising were used to educate the public, and part-time game wardens were hired to protect the swans in their wintering areas. Nevertheless, by 1932, the eastern trumpeter flocks had been exterminated and the western flocks greatly depleted. At last efforts paid off, and the trumpeters were given rare and endangered status both in the United States and Canada. The state of Montana even offered a reward for information concerning illegal hunting of trumpeter swans.

In 1933 the United States breeding population numbered only sixty-nine birds and was restricted to Yellowstone National Park and nearby areas such as Red Rock Lakes in southwestern Montana (which was to be established two years later as the Red Rock Lakes Migratory Waterfowl Refuge). The Red Rock Lakes flock grew with the establishment of the 40,000-acre refuge in 1935. Within three years the population had doubled to ninety-eight, and by 1944 it had jumped to 207. The figure stood at 417 in 1951, and since then the population has stabilized with about 500 birds producing 100 cygnets a year.

Six trumpeter swans were removed in 1955 from the Red Rock Lakes flock to the Delta Waterfowl Research Station in Manitoba. Stock from Red Rock Lakes has also been transferred to the National Elk Refuge in Wyoming, the Malheur National Wildlife Refuge in Oregon, Ruby Lake National Wildlife Refuge in Nevada, and the Lacreek National Wildlife Refuge in South Dakota.

The aim of this transplanting program was to supply the nucleus of a new population to many available habitats still to be found in the Northwest in the hopes of re-establishing the swans in some of their old areas. The trumpeter swans have nested successfully in all the above-mentioned locations. The newly established Manitoba birds started to produce young in 1959, with broods having been raised each year since then. There was particular cause for celebration when the first cygnets were hatched at Lacreek in 1963, because these were the first trumpeter swans to hatch east of the United States Rockies in eighty years.

Red Rock Lakes Refuge lies in the east end of Montana's Centennial Valley, about fifty miles west of Yellowstone National Park. This valley is a broad trough between two high mountain ranges, whose towering peaks are snow-capped the year round.

The run off from the snow, as well as numerous springs and streams, provide a steady supply of water to the lakes and marshes. The area is an ideal habitat for the trumpeter swan and was probably used by them long before man came to North America.

Because of hot water springs on the Red Rock Lakes Refuge, some of the lakes and springs do not freeze over in the winter, and most of the swans do not migrate except for short trips across the range to the north fork of the Snake River in Idaho. The fact that these trumpeter swans do not make the long, dangerous trip to distant wintering grounds, has helped to reduce illegal shooting and other threats to the safety of these magnificent large birds. The refuge management gives the swans supplementary feedings during the winter months, and protects their nesting sites from harmful disturbances by intruders during the summer nesting season.

By 1967 there were estimated to be 1,500 or more trumpeter swans throughout Canada and the United States. A winter feeding program at Lonesome Lake in British Columbia, under the supervision of the Canadian Wildlife Service, resulted in an increase in swan numbers from thirty-five in 1935 to 515 during the winter of 1970-71. Efforts are being made to disperse some of these birds because of the limited natural habitat at Lonesome Lake to lakes and estuaries along the British Columbia coast.

Some 3,000 trumpeter swans now nest in Alaska and winter on coastal lakes and rivers in the southernmost parts of Vancouver Island in severe winters. Another 400 to 500 birds nest in the Red Rock Lakes and Yellowstone National Park area of Montana, and winter in the Red Rock Lakes National Wildlife Refuge or on the headwaters of the Snake River, where feeding areas are kept open by warm springs during the cold winter weather. Approximately 100 birds, which breed near Grande Prairie, Alberta, make up the only significant nesting population of trumpeter swans in Canada. These winter with the Red Rock Lakes birds on the headwaters of the Snake River. Further growth of the Grande Prairie population is restricted by a shortage of suitable nesting habitat and the large territory required by each breeding pair. All but two of approximately thirty-five nesting lakes are smaller than 800 acres, the maximum territory that can be protected by a pair of trumpeters. Thus the area can support no more than thirty-six breeding pairs

54

in any one year, and the loss of even one nesting territory will jeopardize the survival of that small population.

Although trumpeter swans have occasionally been observed in the Cypress Hills region of southwestern Saskatchewan over the years, there were no nesting records until 1949, when one brood was reported. Two or three pairs have nested in that region almost every year since then. Two or three other pairs have occasionally raised broods near Brooks, Alberta over the years.

Despite its former wide distribution, this species is rather specialized in its requirements for breeding habitat. Like whooping cranes, each pair of trumpeter swans requires a large territory in which to nest. It needs bodies of fresh water that are shallow, quiet, and suitable in level, and that have marshy edges of sedge, cattail or bullrush. The three to nine off-white eggs are deposited on a platform of dead aquatic vegetation on a shoreline or mound. Muskrat houses are favourite nesting sites.

Unlike the whistling swans, which nest in the Arctic regions and make long migrations to wintering grounds in the southern United States, trumpeter swans are comparatively sedentary birds. They breed in more southerly regions and winter as far north as they can find open water and adequate feeding grounds. The young birds remain with their parents throughout the winter and accompany them back to the nesting grounds in late April. The old breeding pairs gradually return to the same nesting lakes used in former years.

Efforts are continuing to restore the trumpeter swan to its former breeding range. If the program of transplanting is to succeed, however, former breeding marshes must be saved. Continued vigilance and the determination of an informed public is needed to prevent unnecessary destruction of the swans' breeding habitat. Re-establishment efforts have so far brought the trumpeter swan back to where the total population numbers between 4,500 and 5,000. Accordingly, in 1969, this species was officially removed from the International Union for Conservation of Nature and Natural Resources' list of rare and endangered species.

The saving of the trumpeter swan is one of the brightest pages in the history of wildlife conservation, and is evidence that wise management can in many cases turn what appeared to be impending doom into a cause for celebration.

CHAPTER 5

MUSK OX *Ovibos moschatus*

The musk ox was first described by Henry Kelsey of the Hudson's Bay Company, while exploring that region on June 17, 1689: "Two buffilo ... ill shapen beast. Their body being bigger than an ox ... their Horns not growing like other Beast but joyn together upon their forehead and so come down ye side of their head and turn up till ye tip be even with ye Buts. Their Hair is near a foot long." It confounded early scientists in 1780 when they called it "Ovibos," literally sheep-cow. But it is neither, nor is it closely related to either of these animals; its closest, but still distant, living relative is the takin of China and Tibet.

Stocky and densely furred, musk oxen were in their glory and widest distribution during the Ice Age of the Pleistocene. Their ancestors probably originated on the west tundras of north-central Asia more than half a million years ago, coming to North America across the Bering land bridge about 90,000 years ago. That was the age of giant mammals, when mammoths stomped over icy plains, and woolly rhinoceroses wallowed in the marshes; when beavers were the size of bears and giant elk carried table-sized palmate antlers. Ancient predators stalked this vast and varied prey: dire wolves and sabre-toothed tigers with six-inch fangs.

During the Ice Age, much of Alaska, most of Canada and a part of the continental United States was covered in immense ice sheets. It is believed that musk oxen survived here and, after the retreat of the glaciers, disappeared in Europe and lasted in Siberia until about 2,000 years ago.

The musk ox is native to northern Canada, northwest Greenland and, formerly, the north coast of Alaska. The original Alaskan population was one of the few North American forms for the destruction of which the natives were more responsible than the white man. Few, if any, white men ever saw a musk ox from the original population in northern Alaska, and information on their existence there is based on reports by Eskimos and on the occasional discovery of skeletal fragments that have survived a century or more in the frozen ground. The last survivors, a herd of thirteen, are believed to have been killed by Eskimos in the mid-1850s. The original sparse Arctic population of musk ox in Canada was also heavily exploited during the nineteenth century for meat and hides. Today the musk ox occurs naturally only in Greenland and northern Canada.

Apart from man, the musk ox's principal enemy is the wolf. To protect themselves from wolves, they close together with the cows and calves in the centre and the bulls, with lowered horns, forming an outer defensive ring. In this way they are able to throw off attacking wolves with powerful thrusts of their horns. This excellent tactical measure against predatory mammals, however, proved fatal to the musk ox when man with his long-range weapons appeared on the scene, for it was easy to annihilate a herd that remained stationary in this way.

With the arrival of the white man and his guns, the musk ox was pushed almost to the brink of extinction. Hundreds were shot for food to support the needs of explorers and whalers. In the first years of this century, an estimated six hundred musk oxen were killed by Admiral Peary's expeditions to the Arctic alone. The narratives of explorers indicate that 1,000 were killed on Ellesmere Island and 500 on Melville Island between 1880 and 1917, for the mariners depended on these animals for their survival. Thousands more were killed for their hides by the trappers and hunters of fur trading companies; between 1862 and 1916 the Hudson's Bay

Company handled over 15,000 skins and undoubtedly many other skins were traded outside the company. The capture of calves for zoological gardens involved the killing of all the adults in their protective ring. Absolute protection for the species was not provided until 1917, and by that time the population was extremely low.

Despite the musk oxen's high Arctic home, the animals do not seem as well adapted to the variety of Arctic conditions as caribous, a species with which they share much of their range. Caribous are able to survive in habitats varying from deep forests to the high Arctic, and are nearly as well protected from cold as musk oxen. Their hooves are much enlarged for travelling over snow-covered ground and they may migrate long distances to take advantage of favourable food conditions, or will paw through the deep snow in search of food. Although the musk ox's warm coat ideally protects it against the severe Arctic conditions, it has no defence against unseasonably high temperatures.

Twenty-four-hour exposure to rain or melting snow saturates their underfur, and if the temperature then falls again below freezing, ice forms among the guard hairs. The musk oxen can only shake themselves, which would not remove the mass of ice entangled in their long fur. This may eventually become so heavy that the animals are unable to move, and are at the mercy of wolves and other predators. In these conditions pregnant cows may be so undernourished by the spring as to be unable to calve, while calves of many others may be born prematurely or die from lack of milk. Many young starve to death, as was the case in 1954, when almost an entire herd of young musk oxen is reported to have perished in the aftermath of a particularly heavy snowfall over northeast Greenland. Such climatic hazards may explain why musk oxen have never colonized the more southerly regions of Greenland, where unseasonable thaws frequently occur.

In 1917 the Canadian Wildlife Service put the musk oxen under protection to prevent them from becoming extinct, and since that time their numbers have slowly recovered. In the late 1960s musk oxen were introduced into their former range along Alaska's Arctic coast. These Alaskan musk oxen are the descendants of a group of thirty calves that were transplanted in 1930 from

Greenland to Nunivak Island off Alaska's west coast. In that year there were only about 500 musk oxen on the Arctic mainland whereas, in 1965, there were 1,500, plus 8,390, on the Arctic islands of Canada. Musk ox calves captured in Canada and Greenland have also been transplanted to west Spitzbergen and Dovre Valley in Norway, as well as to Iceland, Nunivak Island, Alaska, and to the Kergulen Islands off Antarctica. Introductions to Sweden, however, have not been successful.

On some of the Arctic islands the numbers of musk oxen have increased enough to permit limited hunting by native peoples. Beginning in 1970, the Eskimos of Banks and Ellesmere Islands were permitted to kill a total of twenty musk oxen each year, and sport hunting has been proposed as a means of increasing the income of some northern communities. In February 1972, the Northwest Territories Council also voted to permit the hunting of thirty-two musk oxen in the territory each year. However, public opposition and some scathing press comments scotched the plan; even hunters agree that to march up to a stationary musk ox and shoot it down could hardly be called sport.

The Alaska Department of Fish and Game in co-operation with the U.S. Bureau of Sport Fisheries and Wildlife are managing the musk ox population in Nunivak National Wildlife Refuge. Originally the herd was fully protected there but, as it reached the limit of its food supply, population control measures became imperative. The immediate, but temporary, solution to controlling the population was to transplant excess animals to their original ranges in Arctic Alaska. If the productivity of the Nunivak herd is maintained, additional animals will become surplus and transplants will be continued, thus further enriching the Arctic environments.

Domestication programs for musk oxen have been established in Alaska and at Fort Chimo near Ungava Bay in Quebec. The intention has been to create native industries based on the manufacture of clothing and other items from the wool of the musk ox, which provides one of the finest natural fibres known to man.

In 1970 there were twenty-three knitting villages around Fort Chimo, where the Eskimo women knitted a large, one-ounce scarf each week which sold for $25. The initial Fort Chimo group of twelve females and three male calves was obtained by separating the young from the adults in a wild herd and then flying the young animals off in helicopters. The Fort Chimo herd of thirty is now thriving, and such herds can also be established commercially in other villages.

Fred Bruemmer, in his book, *Encounters with Arctic Animals*, relates the fact that musk oxen cannot be shorn like sheep; instead the wool must be lifted off. Musk oxen begin to shed their under-wool in May and June, when it comes off in sheets and works its way through the stiff outer guard hairs. At this time musk oxen tend to look rather motheaten and ragged, as they rub themselves against boulders and cliffs to rid themselves of the thick, brownish wool. With the domesticated musk ox the wool is simply lifted off the animal as it comes loose, and the musk ox, whose skin is itchy at this time, loves to be scratched and petted, parting willingly with its wool. The musk ox produces about six pounds of *qivrut* each summer in comparison to a cashmere goat which produces only six ounces of *pashm* a year.

Today, of Canada's 10,000 or so musk oxen, approximately 8,500 are found on the Arctic islands, especially Banks and Elles-mere Islands. About one third of a mainland population of approximately 1,500 are located in the Thelon Game Sanctuary, which was established in 1927, just north of the tree-line, specifically for the musk oxen's protection.

The areas north of Great Bear Lake, around Bathurst Inlet, and in northeastern Keewatin, are other important musk ox ranges on the mainland. Through aerial surveys, tagging and radio-tracking programs, and studies of range conditions, Canadian Wildlife Service biologists are monitoring the state of musk ox populations to ensure that the increasing activity in the north is not having any adverse effects on the species.

With the continued use of these protective measures, the musk ox will almost certainly never again face the threat of extinction.

CHAPTER 6

PRONGHORN *Antilocapra americana*

"Many of us experience a feeling of guilt when we think of what our forefathers did to the bison and the pronghorn," declares Joe Van Wormer in *The World of the Pronghorn*. "Although we were not around at the time and played no part in the wholesale killing of these animals, we assume some of the responsibility, partly as an inheritance and partly because we suspect that, had we been there we, too, would have participated in their destruction."

For a million years the pronghorn has roamed the plains and deserts of North America in substantially the same form; fossil remains indicate that all its ancestors were North Americans, and apparently none ever left their native shores. They formerly ranged from southern Saskatchewan west to the Pacific slopes and south to the plateaus of Mexico, frequenting prairies, sagebrush plains, deserts, and tablelands. In their heyday they were thought to have approached a population of 40 to 50 million, and roamed in huge herds that in numbers even rivalled the plains bison. But by 1924 the total population is estimated to have declined to about 13,000 individuals.

The Lewis and Clark expedition of 1804-06 brought back a specimen from which George Ord, a zoologist of the period,

derived the animal's scientific name "Antilocapra," meaning goat-antelope. Although called antelope erroneously, the pronghorn is neither an antelope nor a goat, but has derived from a distinct and separate family of animals that has been evolving on this continent for 20 million years. The Spanish explorer, Francisco Vasquez Coronado, is assumed to have been the first white man to see the pronghorn, when, in 1540, he made a trip north from Mexico, through what is now New Mexico, and into Kansas. It is reported that he described pronghorns as "stags patched with white."

Unlike the deer, moose, elk, bighorn sheep, and bison, which are all believed to have migrated to this continent from Asia in prehistoric times, the pronghorn is the only hoofed animal that is truly indigenous to North America. This uniqueness is compounded by their being the only mammal with horns that are shed annually. The horn of the pronghorn – possessed by both sexes – is composed of a hollow sheath over a bony core. It arises from the skull directly above the eyes and has one forward-pointing prong about halfway up its length. The tip curves back. Other mammals with true horns, such as cattle, sheep, goats, musk ox, and antelopes, retain their horns throughout their life.

The pronghorn is a relatively small, hoofed herbivore with bucks averaging about 115 pounds and does slightly more than ninety. The upper parts of the body are a rich tan, while the rump, underparts, and two bands across the neck, are pure white. Since pronghorns cover wide areas of climatic fluctuations where temperatures may range from over 100 degrees Fahrenheit in summer to fifty below zero in winter, they have to be able to regulate their body temperature. They are dependent on a very fine under fur, with most of the hairs being relatively thick, tubular structures containing large air cells which form layers of insulation.

While feeding, pronghorns are extremely alert and can detect the approach of predators from a great distance. When alarmed, they elevate the white hairs of their rump patch, which appears to serve as a warning signal to other members of their group. This white patch is extremely distinctive and can be seen from a long way off. On top of that, in its excitement, the pronghorn exudes a musky odour from its scent glands that can be smelled by another animal grazing a full mile away. That odour and those flashing white hairs are relayed across the flat land until every pronghorn for miles is alerted.

Predators did not contribute to the pronghorn's decline because few can catch it. The pronghorn is said to be the swiftest animal in North America and probably second only to the cheetah in all the world, having been clocked under favourable circumstances, running at more than sixty miles an hour. To supply all the oxygen required for such high-powered bursts of exertion, the animal has an unusually large windpipe, measuring a full five inches around. Another of the pronghorn's primary defence mechanisms is its extraordinary vision. Its eyeball is as large as that of a horse, measuring one and a half inches across and set in the socket so as to give the animal a wide-angled view. These eyes are said to be equivalent to the human eye, aided by seven-power binoculars.

The pronghorn's speed and elusiveness so impressed the early Indians that they vested the animal with supernatural powers. They referred to the pronghorn as the phantom of the prairie where the animal roamed free in gigantic herds.

That freedom ended abruptly when the white settlers arrived with their long rifles. Commercial hunters found a ready market for pronghorn meat in the new cities of the West, where in some areas, in 1850, pronghorn steaks sold for 25 cents a pound. In view of the fact that the meat of the pronghorn is considered among the tenderest and tastiest of any of the hoofed animals' – superior to prime beef – it is not surprising that this beautiful animal should have been so mercilessly hunted until its extinction seemed imminent.

Those animals that did survive the onslaught were forced to share their increasingly limited grazing ground with domestic sheep and cattle. Farmers and ranchers further plowed the pronghorn's feeding grounds in a continuation of the indiscriminate slaughter of the herds which they feared would compete with their livestock.

In 1859, drought in one area of southern California forced pronghorns to concentrate at a water source – a location that can make them particularly vulnerable because of their predictable presence. One old trapper-hunter took advantage of the situation and built himself a brush blind nearby. From this hidden vantage point, he slaughtered some 5,000 pronghorns. He took only the hides; the carcasses were left to rot.

In 1881, over 55,000 hides were shipped down the Yellowstone River to St. Louis, Missouri. Without a doubt, it was man alone that caused the near extinction of the pronghorn, beginning with the settling of the West in the 1880s. The contributing factors were: relentless hunting pressures; the fencing of prairies, which destroyed the pronghorn's freedom of movement to feeding and breeding grounds; extensive plowing and planting of virgin prairies; some competition from livestock; and severe winters.

The winter of 1906-7 was a very severe one and many of the herds were completely wiped out. It is estimated that at that time there were less than 2,000 pronghorns left in Canada, and less than 20,000 throughout the entire continent, where once they had numbered in the millions. In the 1920s the pronghorn was well on the road to extinction.

Around that time, however, public attitudes towards wildlife conservation started to change and state game agencies throughout the West began putting full-time wardens into the field. Soon, hunting laws were being enforced, and the wholesale slaughter of the pronghorn was brought to a halt. Also, homesteading declined throughout much of the animal's range as weary prairie farmers gave up their unprofitable business and moved to the cities, thus returning much of the pronghorn's usurped habitat. In addition, in 1922, Nemiskam National Park was established in southern Alberta to preserve a small herd of forty-two pronghorns on a 5,000-acre fenced range. These events resulted in rapid growth of the pronghorn population, which by 1932, had increased to approximately 68,000 in the United States and to 2,400 in Canada.

In 1931, the Boone and Crockett Club and the National Audubon Society acted together to purchase some 34,000 acres in northwestern Nevada and set it aside as the Sheldon National Antelope Refuge. Five years later, President Franklin Delano Roosevelt set aside an additional half-million acres of adjacent public land as the Charles Sheldon Antelope Range, and at the same time created the Hart Mountain National Antelope Refuge in nearby southeastern Oregon. Together, these three areas provided (and still do) needed breeding, fawning, and wintering areas for the pronghorns of the region.

Since then, as a result of closed hunting seasons and the pronghorns' own adaptability to modern range conditions, their numbers have steadily increased. In March 1966, the government ruled that ranchers who graze cattle on public lands cannot put up barbed-wire fences. The results have been dramatic. Pronghorns have increased over 1,000 per cent and are now hunted in fourteen western United States. Close to one million pronghorns have been harvested in the last fifty years, according to Jim Yoakum, biologist for the U.S. Bureau of Land Management in Nevada.

Today the species remains strong and healthy, with a total population of about 435,000, and the biggest herds concentrated on the west side of the Rocky Mountains in Nevada, Oregon, and California. They are now even fairly numerous in Wyoming and Montana, and in southeastern Alberta and southwestern Saskatchewan, where limited hunting has also been permitted in recent years. Of the five recognized subspecies of pronghorns, only the peninsula pronghorn *Antilocapra americana peninsularis* from Baja California, and the smaller and paler Sonoran pronghorn *A.a. sonoriensis* from southern Arizona, and the state of Sonora in Mexico, are currently listed as endangered.

However, protective measures on behalf of the Sonoran pronghorn have already been taken with the establishing of Cabeza Prieta Game Range and Organ Pipe Cactus National Monument in Arizona. The Mexican government is also taking protective measures on the pronghorn's Mexican range, where the animal is believed to be confined to northwest Sonora from about 100 miles northwest of Hermosillo, north to the Pinacate region. The small numbers of Sonoran pronghorn in the United States are dependent for survival on the existence of a larger nucleus on the Mexican side of the border; in some years, no specimens are found on the American side. This makes the Sonoran pronghorn a mammal of international interest, whose future survival will depend on cooperation between the United States and Mexico.

The present pronghorn situation is clearly improved over that at the turn of the century, and the return of these herds is an important credit to the efforts of wildlife management in North America.

CHAPTER 7

HUDSONIAN GODWIT *Limosa haemastica*

The sudden decline of the passenger pigeon in the 1880s created a void in the market for edible North American birds. Attention was turned to many species of native shore birds. Mass destruction of these birds was carried out on such a gigantic scale that within two decades, all but the smaller birds were reduced almost to the brink of extinction.

Those especially victimized included the American golden plover, long-billed curlew, upland sandpiper, and the Hudsonian godwit. Extinction was predicted for all these species. Except for the almost extinct Eskimo curlew, the others still remain with us, although not one of these birds has been able to regain its numbers of former years. The Hudsonian godwit, however, is the only one to have been placed on the International Union for Conservation of Nature and Natural Resources' list of endangered species.

The Hudsonian godwit had suffered everywhere on its migratory routes. As this species, like the Eskimo curlew, followed a long and perilous migration route, off Canada's coast in the fall and through the interior in the spring, it cannot be stated with certainty that its decline was not in part contributed to by shooting on its South American wintering grounds.

Aborigines on their northern breeding grounds ate them in certain quantities, and Labrador and Newfoundland fishermen salted them down in numbers during their arduous flight, when they were especially plump and delicious. Prior to this era of intensive market hunting, shore birds were usually taken only in small numbers by wealthy sporting types.

A large, handsome, bird, the female godwit is about sixteen inches in length, the male smaller by one and a half to two inches. The most characteristic feature is the long, slightly upturned bill. In spring plumage, the Hudsonian godwit can be recognized easily at almost any distance by the rich reddish or brownish plumage, darker on the upperside, and by the conspicuous white rump and black tail. The winter plumage is grey. The axillars are jet black and the wing lining is black. An immature bird, while standing, might be mistaken for a willet, but it is a much slenderer bird and has a longer, thinner, bill. The Hudsonian godwit is the North American counterpart of the Eurasian black-tailed godwit, a species which has appeared as an occasional straggler to our shores.

In the fall, the godwits gather in flocks on the western shores of Hudson Bay, preparing for their eastward migration to the Atlantic coasts of the Maritime provinces and New England. The species is said to decoy readily and to be easily lured by a good imitation of its call, though more wary and cautious than most shore birds if it suspects danger. It is currently believed that on leaving the Hudson Bay area, the species flies non-stop across Ontario and New England to the east coast and south along the Atlantic en route to the more remote regions of the Argentine pampas. This constitutes a vast distance of over 4,000 miles from the birds' breeding area in northern Canada.

Less is known about the Hudsonian godwit's spring migration. It would appear to cross western Ontario, the prairie provinces, and southern Mackenzie, where it disperses somewhat along the shore areas and borders of lakes and rivers. Those flocks spotted in the southern United States have invariably been small, thereby proving an effective defence against sport hunting. This species has been officially reported during migration on South Island, New Zealand, an event which still goes unexplained.

Little is known of the homelife and preferred habitat of the Hudsonian godwit during the nesting period, but probably it occurs on the borders of lakes and ponds on the tundra. Two discrete populations are known: one in the Mackenzie River delta, and quite recently (since 1947) in the Churchill area of Hudson Bay in Manitoba. Rumour has it that it may breed in Keewatin, in the interior of Southampton Island, and perhaps on the peninsula south of that large island; also, possibly on Akimiski Island in James Bay, and in Franklin in the Cumberland Sound area of Baffin Island.

The historical picture of the Hudsonian godwit shows an astonishing parallel to that of the Eskimo curlew. The nest, for instance, was first found by the original discoverer of the Eskimo curlew's nest near Fort Anderson in Mackenzie District, by Roderick MacFarlane on June 9, 1862.

Its present survival status differs from that of the Eskimo curlew as it has been officially regarded as out of danger since 1958, after a long period in which it was thought to be rapidly declining.

Of the six endangered bird species specifically mentioned in Franklin Delano Roosevelt's National Resources Treaty of 1941, the godwit is one of two species that has recovered and is out of danger. The other is the trumpeter swan. Perhaps the godwit survived the shooting pressures on the Central and Atlantic flyways of North America in the nineteenth and early twentieth centuries because it was never as tame or trusting as the vulnerable Eskimo curlew.

The Hudsonian godwit would appear to have had a somewhat chequered past. Relevant literature strongly suggests that this species has never been plentiful, and was originally perhaps the rarest of all our shore birds, even before the heyday of the market hunter. Many ornithologists have never seen it in life.

All early writers reported it as uncommon or rare. Audubon referred to it as "of rare occurrence in any part of the United States." He never saw it in life, and handled only a few market specimens in the flesh. E.A. Preble saw a number of godwits on the beach about fifty miles north of York Factory in Manitoba as early as July 19, 1900; these birds were last seen by him below Cape Churchill, Manitoba, on August 24 of the same year.

On August 13, 1903, large numbers of godwits occurred on the Long Island coast, where many were killed. That had been the only record for a flight of Hudsonian godwits for that locality in seven years. Two weeks later only seven were killed, and subsequent godwits were taken only singularly or in pairs. Dr. L.C. Sanford described a hunting trip to the Magdalen Islands in the Gulf of St. Lawrence, also in 1903:

> At high water they congregate on the upper beaches well out of reach of any disturber. For a long time it was impossible to average a blind in the range of the flight, but finally, by piling up heaps of seaweed and stalking them down far out in the shallow water, we managed to kill a small number. They quickly learned the danger, however, and would keep on their course, just out of reach.

Ernest Gibson reported that prior to 1920 Hudsonian godwits were very abundant in numerous flocks, some of over 1,000 in the area of Buenos Aires, Argentina. Gibson stated the following:

> On more than one of these occasions several birds have dropped to my gun. The flock would then again and again sweep round and hover over the individuals in the water, uttering loud cries of distress, quite regardless of my presence in the open and renewed gunfire. Though the godwit is such an excellent table bird, I found myself unable to continue under these circumstances. I might select my birds but so closely were they packed together that the shots went practically "into the brown" and caused innumerable cripples.

However, the late ornithologist Arthur Cleveland Bent considered the Hudsonian godwit to be "almost extinct" in the 1920s, and Dr. Alexander Wetmore of the Smithsonian Institution reported in 1921 on the dramatic decrease of the godwit population: "The passing of this fine bird must be a cause of great regret among nature lovers alike, to be attributed to the greed of gunners and to the fact that its large size and gregarious habits made it desirable to secure and when opportunity offered easy to kill in large numbers. There is little hope even under the most vigorous protection that the species can regain its former numbers."

Official bird listings published in 1936 indicated the Hudsonian godwit as being extinct, although six years previously, Canadian naturalists Percy Taverner and A.C. Lloyd observed ten pairs of these birds on the western shore of Hudson Bay. They were unable to find any nests, however. The species was again sighted by bird artist Terence Shortt, and C.E. Hope, while camping at Moosonee, Ontario, on July 25, 1942. Shortt and Hope are credited with having seen an estimated 1,200 of these birds, which is far more than has been seen on this continent since the beginning of the present century. The godwits, in the process of early migration, were also accompanied by huge flocks of knots, whimbrels, and other shore birds. From this we can only conclude that the Hudsonian godwit has all along been considerably more common than authorities were given to believe.

Further to the godwit's rediscovery, Hazel R. Ellis, from Cornell University's Department of Ornithology, found a Hudsonian godwit's nest in 1947 at Churchill, Manitoba. The nest contained three eggs, all of which hatched successfully on July 8 of that year. More nests were subsequently found by Canadian ornithologist Leslie Tuck in 1961, and in the following year J.A. Hagar began a study of Hudsonian godwit nesting in the Churchill area, which has greatly contributed to the knowledge of this little-known bird's breeding habits.

Signs of recovery continued throughout the 1950s with the ability of hunters to identify protected birds in North America. In 1956, 370 Hudsonian godwits were seen together on their spring passage at Squaw Creek, Missouri, and transit flocks were improving in size in several national wildlife refuges in the United States. Small numbers of this species have also been observed travelling north through the Mississippi Valley. Since their winter quarters remain relatively unknown, it may be that they have found some haven that agriculturalists and hunters have overlooked.

Happily, the upward trend continues and it may now be possible for most bird watchers to add this handsome bird species to their life list.

CHAPTER 8

POLAR
BEAR *Ursus maritimus*

The great white bear inhabits the Arctic regions of both the Old and New World. It rivals in size the great Kodiak bear of Alaska, the largest living carnivore; there have been authenticated reports of polar bears weighing up to 1,600 pounds. The shape of the polar bear is quite different from that of the Kodiak bear, however. Its body, especially the neck and legs, is much longer and it has a long narrow head and very small ears. Its foot pads are covered with fur; its claws and tongue are black, its eyes are dark brown.

In North American Arctic coastal regions it ranges from the Seward Peninsula in Alaska east to Labrador, and south along the shores of Hudson and James Bays, where it preys mainly on the ringed seal *Phoca hispida*, and to a lesser degree on the bearded seal *Erignathus barbatus*.

This bear is the most carnivorous of all the family, being extremely skillful at catching seals. It may wait beside a hole in the ice and kill the seal when it comes up to breathe, or it may stalk its prey. If there is no cover to offer concealment, the polar bear will crawl on its belly until it is close enough to rush and kill the seal with a blow of its huge paw. In addition to seals, the food of the polar bear consists of fish, shrimp, molluscs, foxes, caribou,

birds, lemmings, young walrus, and an occasional whale that is washed ashore or trapped in shallow water. When polar bears are on land they eat some grasses and roots, with seaweed sometimes being added.

During the last glaciation the polar bear lived south of its present range. In 1690, Von Siebold, a German naturalist, reported that polar bears reached the northern island of Japan, and they were once more common in the Bering Strait and Iceland than they are now. Most people think of the polar bear as having always lived at the North Pole and nowhere else. Actually, the North Pole is too far north for even a polar bear. However, individual bears have been seen in the frozen Arctic Ocean as far as eighty-eight degrees latitude North, only two degrees from the North Pole. A most unusual record was that of an old female that was shot near Peribonca, Lake St. John District in Quebec, on or about October 29, 1938.

The almost total absence of polar bears on the Canadian Arctic islands is due to the fact that the inshore ice of those coasts does not break up every summer and provide suitable areas of open water for seals, causing them to migrate to other areas where fresher ice and open water are available. Conversely, where the ice-pack is constantly moving, often breaking up even in winter, as is the case off Alaska and the northeastern coast of Greenland, the conditions are peculiarly suited to the requirements of seals, and polar bears are more common on these coasts than in most other parts of the Arctic.

It can therefore be seen that the distribution of the polar bear is also governed by its need for land during part of each year, particularly when seals are scarce and alternative sources of food must be found, as well as during the denning period. At that time they will feed upon walrus, fish, sea birds, and stranded whales. These ecological requirements mean that actual land used by the bear is a relatively small portion of the vast Arctic regions.

Polar bears are generally thought to have been more abundant in the past than they are today. For thousands of years they were hunted by Eskimos using dogs and spears, and they were an essential Arctic resource. While not feared, "Nanook," as the Eskimos called the white bear, was treated with respect for its courage, cunning, and great strength. The hides and meat of polar bears have for centuries constituted a substantial proportion of the income and food of Eskimos and bear hunting is still important to many Canadian and Greenland Eskimos. With the introduction of firearms, however, large numbers were taken.

Depletion of polar bears by successive waves of explorers, whalers, sealers, and fur traders, since the seventeenth century have caused concern for their future survival. At first they were killed only occasionally for their fur and meat, but with the decline of whaling one hundred years ago the whalers turned their attention extensively to seals and thus also to the polar bears which competed with them for these animals, notably in the eastern Canadian Arctic and the Greenland Sea.

Polar bears, once secure in their Arctic wilderness, protected as they were by the natural barrier of severe environmental conditions and lack of good transportation to the region, have faced the threat of increased hunting from aircraft and motor toboggans. Bears were hunted for sport, captured for zoos and killed for their meat and luxurious pelt. From 1920 to 1930 alone Norwegian hunters killed about 700 polar bears a year on Spitzbergen; between 1945 and 1963 about 6,000 bears were killed. In Canada about 600 were killed annually. Alaska made a profit of about $450,000 from 292 polar bears killed in 1965. A pronounced decline in the species continued through the 1930s, particularly in Greenland, and especially along the western and southeastern coasts.

The popularity of polar bear hunting had reached a peak in the early 1960s. The Boone and Crockett Club (whose founder was Theodore Roosevelt) is the arbiter and record-keeper of North American big-game hunting. Some measure of the interest in polar bear hunting can be found in the record book published in 1964. Of the twenty-five largest polar bears known to the records of big-game hunters, fourteen have been killed since 1960.

It once was something of an accomplishment to hunt and kill a polar bear armed only with a rifle of questionable ballistic performance. It was a man-sized task and more than one hunter lost his life in the attempt. But more recent methods of hunting the bear with the use of two planes, a guide, a pack of sled dogs and high-powered rifle, have eliminated the element of risk to the hunter.

In 1955, the International Union for the Conservation of Nature General Assembly recommended that the polar bear be protected. Russia banned all hunting of them two years later, but in Canada about 600 bears were still killed each year for twelve recurrent years, despite the decrease in their population, which occurred mostly in the high Arctic.

A notable initial step to save the polar bear was the First International Conference on Polar Bears, held at the University of Alaska in Fairbanks on September 16, 1965. The conference invited the IUCN to accept responsibility for collecting scientific data on polar bear research.

It is now known that most of the world's polar bears are in Canada, possibly 10,000 to 12,000 occurring here. In 1964 about 600 bears, nearly half of the world's kill of 1,300, were taken in the Canadian Arctic. But in 1965 in Alaska alone 300 bears were killed. In 1967, the Northwest Territories adopted a quota system in an effort to reduce the take of bears by each Eskimo village, although in 1970, the Canadian quota was 415 bears to be shot by Eskimos, but this could not be effectively enforced and many animals were killed illegally as well. The world kill apparently reached a peak of about 1,500 in 1968 and 1969, but is currently coming under better control.

In Canada the need for more research on polar bears became apparent by the late 1950s. Oil exploration in the Arctic was becoming increasingly widespread and many Inuit were becoming owners of snowmobiles. The price of polar bear skins began to climb and so, in turn, did the numbers killed. The recorded kill in 1960 in Canada was 509 compared to 277 in 1950 and 148 in 1940. The known kill was over 700 in 1968. In 1972 the going price for a polar bear was $70 per foot, with some stretched hides measuring over ten feet.

Although polar bear hunting for bounty payments in Canada is predominantly an Inuit activity, in 1970 the government of the Northwest Territories approved an ordinance allowing limited sport hunting by non-residents, guided by Inuit hunters, with the purpose of bringing more money into the community. The total number of bears killed does not in this way increase because each animal taken by a non-resident hunter is included in the settlement quota. The $2,500 fee is distributed among the guides and other members of the community and is more money than could be obtained by simply selling a hide, say, for $400 to $700; therefore many people benefit from the killing of the bear. The hunt is regulated as a "quality product," and the use of set-guns or motorized transport of any kind is prohibited.

Since polar bears have on the average only two young, and don't breed until three or four years old, recovery of depleted populations is slow. Stricter regulations and tighter controls have now been applied in many regions. Increased international interest in the welfare of the polar bear has been evident since 1965, when the five Arctic countries – Canada, the United States, Denmark, Norway, and the Soviet Union – met to exchange information and ideas. These countries meet every two years under the auspices of the International Union for the Conservation of Nature and Natural Resources to discuss the results of current research and to co-ordinate future plans.

In November 1973, Canada, Denmark, Norway, and the United States, signed an agreement for the conservation of polar bears, with the Soviet Union signing in February 1974. The agreement provides for better collaboration among the Arctic nations in the research and management of polar bears. In particular, it prohibits hunting of polar bears in international waters, and outlaws hunting on land with the use of aircraft or other motorized vehicles. Hunting of polar bears in Canada is solely restricted to native people, who hunt the bear with the aid of sled-dogs. Further, the establishment of the 7,000-square-mile Polar Bear Provincial Park in 1970 by the Ontario government was a heartening step forward.

There are few documented cases of deliberate attacks on man by polar bears, though there is seldom an opportunity to conduct an adequate investigation. However, the 1966 attack on a boy near Fort Churchill, Manitoba, provided such a chance. The bear was sought out and killed. During the autopsy Dr. Charles Jonkel, research scientist for the Canadian Wildlife Service, found that the bear had been wounded with firearms earlier in the year and had again on the day of the attack. The earlier wound had driven a canine tooth into the nasal passage, blinding at least one eye. Thus, the attack was not unprovoked. The attack on two Indians in 1967 was also found to have been indirectly provoked, though evidence was less conclusive than in the 1966 case. It is believed that the attacking bear had been repeatedly stoned, photographed, fed, and chased with dogs and automobiles.

Dr. Jonkel reported another, this time fatal, attack on a young Eskimo in 1968, just outside Fort Churchill, where the bears had given no previous indication of being dangerous. The boy and several companions saw the tracks of two bears bypassing the settlement along the Hudson Bay coast. They decided to follow the tracks through the snow, and one boy approached too close to where a bear was bedded in a protected area. An autopsy disclosed that the bear had garbage in its stomach but no physical anomalies. This tragic accident, ending in the death of both the boy and the bear, could so easily have been avoided.

The Canadian Wildlife Service, in co-operation with the government departments from provinces and territories within which polar bears occur, have been conducting research studies on this species. Bears are being live-trapped and immobilized with tranquillizing drugs so they can be tagged and even fitted with radio transmitters fastened in collars, and followed over long distances with airplanes. In this way, more can be learned about these animals, whose movements during most of the year remain a mystery.

Surveys along the coasts of Manitoba and Ontario during the past sixteen or seventeen years have shown that in the south coast lowland region, from Cape Churchill to the south end of James Bay, polar bears are abundant and increasing due in large part to the recent conservation efforts mentioned above. Manitoba's bear population is estimated to be between 750 and 1,000.

Important polar bear denning areas are Melville Bay and Kane Basin in the northwestern and eastern coast of Greenland, the east coast of west Spitzbergen, Edgeoya, and Kong Karls Land in the Norwegian Arctic, Franz Josef Land, and Wrangel Island in the Soviet Arctic, and the southern Banks Island, Simpson Peninsula, eastern Southampton Island, and eastern Baffin Island in the Canadian Arctic. No major denning areas seem to exist in Alaska, but polar bears may den occasionally in the vicinity of its northern and northwestern coasts.

According to Rod Standfield, biologist for the Ontario Ministry of Natural Resources, there may be as many as 600 pairs of polar bears in the James and southern Hudson Bay areas alone, with the greatest concentrations being found during the summer around Cape Henrietta Maria. These bears, in turn, migrate northward in the fall, usually ending up in the Churchill area. In comparison to the status of polar bears elsewhere over much of their circumpolar range, the southern Hudson Bay population is in good condition, and bear numbers are probably increasing. Hudson Bay polar bears seem to be larger than their high Arctic counterparts probably because of a less harsh environment. An annual harvest of about ten to thirty polar bears is made by Cree Indians from Fort Severn, Winisk and Attawapiskat in extreme northern Ontario. A cropping of approximately fifteen polar bears occurs here on an annual basis, which most biologists feel to be acceptable. Some of the kills may be classified as "nuisance," bears, which are shot in defence of property.

The harvest does not appear to jeopardize the southern Hudson Bay population. In fact, in certain areas behavioural problems would seem to indicate that there are perhaps too many of these animals in one place. In the late fall, at Cape Churchill, there may be as many as 200 pairs, possibly the largest concentration of polar bears in the world. In some areas, however, they are considered as "vulnerable" as in Newfoundland, Labrador, Spitzbergen in Norway, and in other parts of the high Arctic.

At least eighty polar bear cubs were born along the Hudson Bay coast of Ontario, according to aerial surveys in the spring of 1976. Today there are more polar bears in existence than there were twenty years ago. Since the animals move widely with the polar ice, often crossing international boundaries and travelling far from land, it is difficult to get an accurate population count. A popular estimate has put the world population at a maximum of 20,000, with the Canadian population at over 10,000. With the general increase in polar bear populations, there is every cause for optimism for the future survival of the great white bear.

CHAPTER 9

AMERICAN ALLIGATOR *Alligator mississipiensis*

Although alligators may once have had worldwide distribution, there are only two widely separated species left: the American alligator and the Chinese alligator *Alligator sinensis*, which is found only in China's upper Yangtze River valley.

Early naturalists described vast numbers of alligators throughout their range in the southeastern United States. DuPratz, writing in 1718, stated that the giant reptiles were everywhere and were generally considered a nuisance and killed whenever the opportunity arose.

Even after two centuries of hunting, alligators were numerous in many areas of coastal Louisiana. Around Avery Island they became so numerous at times that they destroyed cattle, hogs and dogs, and their numbers had to be controlled. E.A. McIlhenny wrote an excellent account of his experiences with alligators, covering the period of 1885 to 1935.

John James Audubon described large numbers of alligators in all of the southeastern states that he explored. He stated that "thousands of the largest size were killed, when the mania of having either shoes, boots, and saddleseats, made of their hides, lasted."

Slaughter of the alligator rivalled that of the bison. At least ten million were killed for their hides between the early 1800s and 1940. Alligator hides were used extensively during the Civil War, and many thousands of these reptiles were killed to meet the demand of a leather shortage. Their greatest decline occurred between that period and the first quarter of the twentieth century. The reason for this decline was unquestionably the hide hunters.

The American alligator has a critical place in the wetland ecology of the southeastern United States. In an area such as the Florida Everglades, where there are periodic droughts, the alligator digs a wallow, or big pool. These wallows often become the only reservoirs for water when all else is dry. Fish, birds, and other small animals live in the alligator wallows and drink from them. It is true that at such times the alligator preys on some of the creatures that it plays host to. But at the same time, without the small havens of water, the toll on wildlife populations would be far greater.

Although the greatest decline of alligator populations occurred near the turn of the century, according to Louisiana wildlife biologist Dr. A.W. Palmisano, they reached their lowest level in Louisiana in the late 1950s. Numbers throughout other portions of their range were also rapidly declining at this time and the situation reached crisis proportions by 1960.

Thus in 1960, Louisiana became one of the first states to attempt to regulate the harvest of alligators by implementing a five-foot size limit and a sixty-day spring season. By 1964, it was obvious that more restrictive measures were required, as the population continued to decline. The season was subsequently closed and it has been illegal to kill alligators in Louisiana since that time. Other southeastern states began to close their hunting season, and in 1969, it was illegal to hunt alligators anywhere in the United States. In 1966, at the urging of concerned individuals, the alligator was placed on the federal list of rare and endangered species.

By this time, localized populations were responding well to management. Protecting and restocking, which was initiated in 1958 in the marshes of southwestern Louisiana, resulted in a dramatic increase in the alligator population. This clearly demonstrates that alligators respond well to protection and management in a localized area, even when surrounding populations may be declining. With the serious reduction of the reptile over much of its range, in spite of closed seasons, the stage was set for the next set of events.

The Southeastern Association of Game and Fish Commissioners organized an Alligator Committee to co-ordinate activities relating to the research and management of the alligator. The American Alligator Council was later formed, composed of representatives of state agencies, conservation organizations, and concerned individuals. Later, the group was joined by those interested in alligator farming and representatives of the reptile products industry. All participants agreed that illegal hunting was a serious threat to the alligator and that effective legislative measures should be adopted.

A major problem was the interstate shipment of illegally taken hides. Alligators taken illegally in Louisiana, for instance, could be shipped to another state and although that state was also closed to alligator hunting, it was impossible to prove the origin of the skins. To stop the interstate traffic in illegal hides, the American Alligator Council effectively supported the adoption of the 1970 Endangered Species Conservation Act, and the amendment to the 1900 Lacey Act, which made it a federal crime to transport in interstate or foreign commerce any alligator, or part thereof. Upon conviction of violation of this law, the fine will not exceed $10,000 or more than one year's imprisonment for each offence. The implementation in 1970 of the amended Lacey Act was hailed as a major accomplishment by all persons concerned with the perpetuation and management of the alligator.

However, what had initially been a logical approach to the management of a resource had become viewed as a case of overreaction. The "Mason-Smith Act," as the New York State Endangered Species Law is termed, made it a crime to import or sell any crocodilian hide or product in the state. The law applied equally to alligators, crocodiles, caymans or any other member of the crocodile family. Had the act covered only those species actually threatened with extinction, it would have been a useful bill. However, it went beyond the amended Lacey Act, and imposed

86

severe restrictions on the United States reptile products industry without appreciably affecting the illegal alligator kill.

This "overreaction" has resulted in the division of members of the American Alligator Council into two factions – the majority, who view the alligator as a renewable resource, which can be useful to man and yet remain a viable aspect of the natural environment, and a small group who consider the alligator a species to be completely protected.

Around 1956, when the annual alligator harvest sharply declined – as did the size of the individual specimens – the nine alligator states were becoming concerned. In Louisiana an apparent increase eased the worry until a closer look showed that the floodwaters of Hurricane Audrey in 1957 had carried thousands of alligators out of refuges and into areas where they had no protection.

One such refuge is the Rockefeller Wildlife Refuge, about sixty miles east of the Texas border, where Ted Joanen, research leader for state refuges, has helped to restore the alligator. He admires the animal and he wants its safety assured. But, like the majority of his management colleagues in Louisiana, he does not believe it is endangered.

Key factors responsible for the high alligator populations in areas of Louisiana are habitat preservation and strict enforcement of existing laws on alligators. As an example of the seriousness with which certain local courts view alligator poaching, a sentence of five years and 165 days' imprisonment was the punishment recently imposed in Cameron Parish on an alligator hunter who had previously been convicted on similar charges. This is possibly the most severe jail sentence ever meted out in Louisiana, or elsewhere, for a violation of game laws.

Through the combined efforts of individuals and agencies, alligator poaching in vast areas of Louisiana has been practically eliminated and populations have increased rapidly. By 1972 state biologists' censuses put the number of alligators in Louisiana at 250,000, and the decision was made to allow "an experimental harvest." Many conservationists, led by the National Audubon Society, protested. The society suggested that the animals be transplanted – rather than killed for their hides – to restock suitable areas from which alligators had vanished. The Louisiana

Wildlife and Fisheries Commission's response was to offer 2,000 alligators to the National Audubon Society.

During the first season of alligator transplants in 1974, Audubon workers captured 500 alligators. Two hundred were sent to Arkansas and 300 to Mississippi, to be released in carefully selected areas. During 1975, 1,000 alligators were transplanted – three-quarters of the stock offered by Louisiana – which cost the society $3,500.

Proposed changes appeared in the Federal Register on July 8, 1975, with the losing of the species' protected status in part of its range. In three parishes of southern Louisiana, the state would be free to establish open alligator hunting seasons. The alligator would also be downgraded from the endangered to the threatened species list in seven states: Alabama, Florida, Georgia, Mississippi, South Carolina, Texas, and the remainder of Louisiana. It would continue to be listed as endangered in North Carolina, Arkansas, and Oklahoma.

Alligator hides, along with the products of other endangered species, have continued to find their way, however, into illegal outlets, despite heavy penalties; in fact, federal officials claim that alligator poaching is actually on the rise. Thousands of lawbreakers each year set out to hunt for alligators. Game wardens do the best they can to apprehend the offenders but the swamps are big and full of hiding places. Most offenders escape, together with their ill-gotten gains.

Poachers are especially active during the summer months when they locate the alligator holes where the victims are concentrated and easily slain. Two poachers, working together, can kill and skin as many as $700- or $800-worth of alligators a night. Only the belly skin of the alligator is used and brings the poacher about $5.25 a foot. The usual way of killing an alligator is with a .22 rifle, which can be easily dismantled and hidden in the event of an investigation. Other weapons used to kill alligators include axes, big fish-hooks, baited with chicken, and hammers to batter them on the back of the head.

The alligator population of the United States has made such a good recovery (a current estimate is a minimum population of 750,000) from the low level to which unbridled hide-hunting had brought it, that in three counties in Louisiana the U.S. Fish and Wildlife Service has been able to remove the species from all federal lists. Alligators are as thick as ever in some places. There are so many alligators in the marshes of southwestern Louisiana (an estimated 200,000), that in the fall of 1976, the U.S. Department of the Interior eased protection of the animal to the extent that the state of Louisiana was permitted to conduct a limited hunt. In parts of Florida alligators have turned up in all sorts of unlikely places, including front lawns, golf courses, swimming pools, schoolyards, and sewers. In Miami, an eight-foot specimen held up traffic at a busy intersection, then bit the leg of a wildlife biologist who was sent to remove it. Another alligator ravaged the famous flamingos at Hialeah racetrack. There are some 8,000 complaints about nuisance alligators in Florida each year. Georgia, Texas, South Carolina, Mississippi, and Alabama now also have sizable numbers of alligators.

Clearly, the alligator is no longer in danger of becoming extinct.

CHAPTER 10

HAWAIIAN GOOSE (nene) *Branta sandvicensis*

It is generally believed that about half a million years ago some geese migrating southward stopped on one or more of the Hawaiian Islands. Whether due to injuries, storms, or other natural forces, part of the flock remained behind and, in isolation, developed into a distinct species, which we now know as the Hawaiian goose. It is one of three species of wildfowl restricted to the Hawaiian Islands.

In the eighteenth century, the Hawaiian goose, commonly called the nene (pronounced nay-nay), was widespread below 9,000 feet sea level on the tropical islands of Hawaii and Maui. By the early 1800s there were known to have been 25,000 of these birds inhabiting these beautiful islands, and few people suspected that the species was in any danger. But by 1780 they had in fact begun to decline due to human intervention. Whaling ships stopped by to load up with large numbers of carcasses of these birds, which made delicious eating. The geese were trusting by nature, as isolated creatures tend to be, and were by no means difficult to hunt. Live birds were also captured and their eggs were taken.

It was, however, the arrival of white settlers in Hawaii that really started the downfall of the species. There is little doubt that

the Polynesians hunted these heavily barred, grey-brown birds in their natural habitats on the volcanic slopes of the islands of Hawaii and Maui, but with nothing like the savagery of the civilized westerner.

When the white man settled these lovely islands, he brought with him many alien species that helped destroy the once great flocks of these handsome birds: mongooses, rats, dogs, goats, sheep, cattle, horses, pigs, asses, and at least six different game birds. All of these conspired to destroy nests, and young birds, as well as the adults, competed for habitat, and competed for food. Ships' crews, traders, and settlers, took thousands of birds, and thousands more were salted down and shipped by clipper to California in a thriving trade that took the gold of the forty-niners in exchange for meat.

Another reason for the species' decline was a four-and-a-half-month hunting season – with a bag limit of six birds – which coincided with nesting activities. The white man was used to shooting during autumn and winter in his temperate home, and saw no reason why tropical game birds should not fit the pattern to which he was accustomed.

Hunting was finally banned in 1911, but by that time there were precious few Hawaiian geese left to benefit from reprieve. The isolated geese were not equipped to survive, as is common with almost all other native Hawaiian birds. Sixty per cent of the Hawaiian avian forms, including at least twelve distinct species, have all disappeared.

Two special factors played major roles in the near destruction of the Hawaiian goose. First, it does not migrate and has probably never left the islands since it evolved into a distinct species. Second, and perhaps more important, it lives and breeds on open lava beds, where some of the twenty-nine known plants which constitute its diet, grow. It is, therefore, especially vulnerable to predators.

Since 1959, when the Hawaiian goose became Hawaii's state bird, it has been rigidly protected. Even so, exotic predators, such as the mongoose, are still a serious threat to the birds' survival. From February until May, some young and adults are likely to be flightless and become especially vulnerable. According to wildlife biologist J. Kear, "The mongoose, for one, will probably never be eliminated, and without strict and constant control of predators on the nesting sites, the wild goose population remains at risk."

A Hawaiian landowner by the name of Herbert C. Shipman became deeply concerned for the fate of the Hawaiian goose, and began raising them in captivity at his home at Keaau on Hawaii. Starting in 1918, with a pair of birds obtained from a friend, he bred a flock of forty-three geese over the next thirty years; some he gave to a game farm at Oahu, some escaped back into the wild, and some died in the 1946 tidal wave that struck the islands. In the meantime, the Hawaiian Board of Agriculture and Forestry had started a similar program in 1927 and had raised a flock of forty-two Hawaiian geese. These specimens were all set free, but all but one of the descendants of these birds had died by 1947.

In 1950, John Yealland, curator of the Severn Wildfowl Trust at Slimbridge, England, brought home with him two of Herbert Shipman's geese (both females) and an additional gander from the Hawaiian Board of Agriculture. By 1955, there were probably more birds in captivity than in the wild, and nearly one third of the world's population of the known forty-two birds were in England. By 1958, the flock of Hawaiian geese in England had increased to seventy-three, testifying to the skill and dedication of the Wildfowl Trust in this marvellous venture.

The Wildfowl Trust (under the auspices of Sir Peter Scott) bred 283 Hawaiian geese between 1952 and 1969. The original gander of the Slimbridge flock, named Kamehameha, was the progenitor of 230 geese up to the time of his death in 1963.

As protection against the accidental loss of the flock through disease or other misadventures, breeding pairs were sent to wildfowl centres in Holland, France, Switzerland, as well as other locations in England, and to the care of Dr. S. Dillon Ripley in Connecticut. The World Wildlife Fund (U.S.) then financed the transfer of thirty Hawaiian geese from Slimbridge to Maui, (where the species had been extinct since the nineteenth century), and Haleakala Crater was declared as a national park by the United States government. This area was considered a safe place to start the birds back on the road to recovery in their natural environment.

A small, wild stock of geese had survived on Hawaii itself and may have numbered thirty-five birds. In 1955, a wild flock of twenty-two geese was sighted. It was the first time in nearly two decades that more than eight Hawaiian geese were ever seen at one time. By 1962, the Hawaiian goose population had increased from fifty to over 400, and by 1965 the number had passed 500, and the population continues to increase.

Shipman's flock, from which the Wildfowl Trust population was built, was derived from a few original inbred pairs. It was therefore felt that an introduction of new stock into Hawaii was essential. A pair of wild Hawaiian geese and one young bird were captured in March 1960 for breeding purposes and taken to Pohakuloa headquarters for the restoration program. Meanwhile, the Hawaiian Board of Agriculture had established another farm in 1949, and from the original two geese and two ganders from Shipman's stock the geese population had also built up. Hawaiian geese were re-established in their old haunts on the slopes of Mauna Kea, Mauna Loa, Hualali, and Haleakala.

In 1964, two sanctuaries, totalling 18,000 acres, were declared in Hawaii, and under intensive management the fiftieth American state's official bird now thrives. During the 1966-1967 season in Hawaii, a record number of fifteen nests and broods were recorded with a total population of twenty-two young, and in July 1971 an adult banded pair of geese were seen on Maui for the first time since their reintroduction, together with three full-fledged goslings.

By 1975, twenty-six pairs of Hawaiian geese existed at the Pohakuloa breeding station of the Hawaii State Department of Land and Natural Resources. In all, a total of 1,446 Hawaiian geese have so far been reared, and 1,061 have been released into four sanctuaries on the island of Hawaii, in addition to 187 on Maui, including 197 from Slimbridge and seven from Connecticut. Also, 180 geese have been distributed on loan to forty zoos and wildfowl breeders in all parts of the world. The United States authorities have since informed the Wildfowl Trust that no more Hawaiian geese need be sent across the ocean, as they are now producing enough birds in Hawaii.

Although hunting of this species was forbidden as far back as 1911, it is clear that the nene could not have survived without this concerted effort on the part of individuals like Herbert Shipman and organizations like the Severn Wildfowl Trust and the World Wildlife Fund (U.S.). "Operation Hawaiian Goose" is a good example of nature conservation in action. What began as a tragedy ended as an undeniable triumph of good sense and sound reasoning.

CHAPTER 11

SEA OTTER *Enhydra lutris*

It has been said that the sea otter's only means of defence against man is its lovableness, and one can hardly watch a colony of these charming, playful, animals frolicking in the sea without falling in love with them. When faced with danger they will try to alert each other before diving to get out of harm's way. Fur traders have long taken advantage of this protective trait by grabbing a defenseless youngster and waiting for its frantic mother to come fearlessly after it.

There are two accepted races of sea otters: the northern sea otter *Enhydra lutris lutris*, from Alaska and the Aleutian Islands, and the southern sea otter *E.1. nereis*, now found only off the coast of California. Superficially, the northern and southern races are identical; the distinction of subspecies is based entirely upon minor cranial differences. The head of the sea otter is roundish, the ears are small, hardly visible above the fur, the eyes black and beady, and the white whiskers resemble those of a cat. Sea otters are much bigger than the typical river otter *Lutra canadensis*, weigh from 50 to 100 pounds, and can attain a length of four and a half feet. One of the most noticeable characteristics of the sea otters is that they are constantly cleaning, grooming, and preening

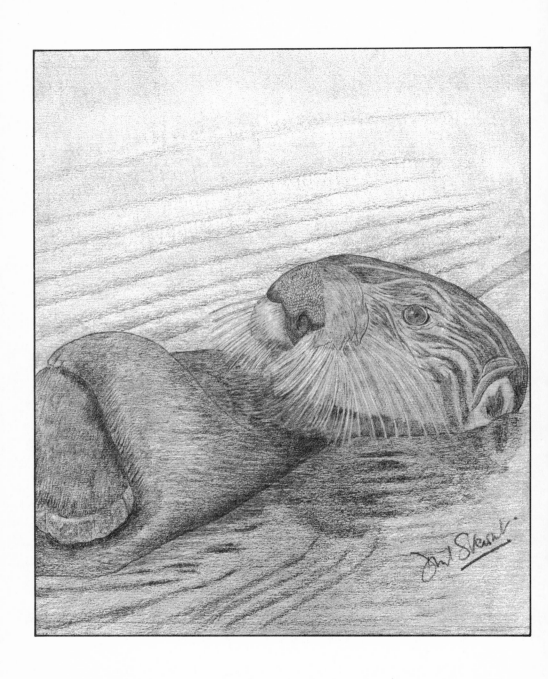

their fur, giving it a rich, luxurious quality. In fact, it was the beauty of this dense, thick, brown fur, tipped with silvery-gold, that almost caused the species to be entirely wiped out.

Sea otters live most of their lives in kelp beds within several hundred yards of shore. They even bear their young in the water and rarely come to land. Unlike other marine mammals, the sea otter floats on its back and maintains this position when swimming on the surface. One of the few animals that uses a tool, it brings up a flat rock from the sea bottom and breaks open snails, sea urchins, crabs, and abalone, by hitting them against the rock.

The animal's ancestry dates back millions of years, when a group of Asiatic land otters probably crossed over the Bering land bridge, and spread down the Pacific coast of North America. Those crab-eating otters first took to the rivers and lakes along the coast, but then, in one of nature's turnabouts, they left the land and went to sea. Slowly adapting to its new salt water environment, the otter grew larger in order to contain its heat in the chilled waters of the Pacific.

Prior to the onset of large-scale hunting in 1741, the year that Vitus Bering, a Danish explorer employed by Russia, discovered the Aleutian Islands, the sea otter ranged from northern Japan throughout the Aleutian Islands, and along the west coast of North America as far south as Morro Hermoso in Baja California.

From the time of their discovery, the northern sea otters were ruthlessly slaughtered. During their first winter in the Aleutians the crew killed hundreds of otters in kelp beds. They ate these marine mammals and used their hides for clothes, rugs, and wall-hangings. They also dried 800 of the skins that first year and later took them back to Russia where they were later to create a great demand. In the three decades between 1790 and 1820 Russian ships were said to have hauled hides of 200,000 otters back across the North Pacific.

In 1867, the United States purchased Alaska from the Russians and the rate of slaughter increased, until in the years between 1881 and 1890 the number killed was at an all-time high, with the Alaska Company taking 47,482 skins. Russian fur hunters, using as helpers the native Aleuts living on the great chain of islands named after them, moved further and further south, as the otter population was decimated in region after region.

Northern sea otters also thrived along the coast of British Columbia before the arrival of the white man. During the last century, though, the price of sea otter pelt rose to $1,000 or more, and these hapless animals were almost hunted to extinction in the province about 1900. The sea otters were so rare that ships that might once have brought back 5,000 were lucky to return with two dozen.

The southern sea otter existed along the coast of California in great numbers during the nineteenth century, but the animal was exploited with such ruthlessness that it was rapidly brought to the point of extinction. The Russians reached California, established Fort Ross in 1812, and within five years are said to have taken 50,000 skins along the Pacific coast; in San Francisco Bay alone the take at times reached 800 animals a week. By 1876, the otter had been exterminated off the Washington and Oregon coasts, and the last specimen in California was reportedly killed in 1911, south of Fort Ord.

This unrestricted and remorseless slaughter of sea otters during the eighteenth and nineteenth centuries eliminated approximately one million sea otters, killed for their fur, and very nearly obliterated the species.

In 1910, the United States government introduced a law prohibiting the capture of sea otters within America's waters, and simultaneously entered into negotiations with other concerned governments for similar protection. When the treaty protecting the otters was signed in 1911, by the United States, the Soviet Union, Japan, and Great Britain, many authorities believed them to be already extinct.

However, after a few years, during which no otters were sighted, some were at last seen around Russia's Commander Island. To the delight of the conservationists, a colony of northern sea otters was also discovered in 1936, off Alaska's Amchitka Island (which was subsequently made part of a wildlife refuge), and happily, two years later, ninety-four specimens of the southern race were seen off Bixby Creek on the Monterey coast of California.

Since this discovery, both populations have thrived with the Alaskan group increasing to about 40,000 to 120,000, while the California population has extended its range southward to Point

Conception and possibly as far as the Channel Islands. There has, however, been only slight expansion northward.

By 1970, owing to the resurgence in their populations, the sea otter fur industry was resurrected and the commercial killing of these animals was reinstated. This continued until November 1971 when President Nixon sanctioned a nuclear explosion on Alaska's Amchitka Island, which virtually wiped out the northern sea otter colony there. Other rare and endangered species, such as bald eagles and peregrine falcons, also perished. Alaskan biologists later determined that most of the local northern sea otter colony – 900 to 1,100 animals – had been killed in the blast.

Prior to the Amchitka nuclear explosion, ninety-one sea otters were transplanted from Alaska to the kelp beds off the west coast of Vancouver Island. At least one young sea otter was reported in 1975 from British Columbia and Oregon, showing that the transplants of Alaskan sea otters to a part of their range where they had become extinct are beginning to succeed. In the meantime, the Amchitka colony has begun to show signs of recovery and commercial killing of otters has not been resumed, since it is now prohibited by law.

The appealing animals have their own pressure group, the Friends of the Sea Otter, to stave off threats from commercial interest. The friends of the animals of the sea persuaded Congress to pass the Marine Mammal Protection Act, signed into law on October 21, 1972. With this law came an indefinite moratorium on the killing of marine mammals except by special permission. There is, however, some opposition from Alaska, which is attempting to have the U.S. Department of the Interior lift the moratorium.

The northern sea otters have been shown to occupy a key position in the coastal ecosystem of the Aleutian Islands. Sea otters feed to a large extent on sea urchins, thereby keeping their numbers under control, and preventing them from overgrazing the kelp and other marine vegetation. Harbour seals *Pusa vitulina* and bald eagles are among the animals whose food is diminished by a reduction in sea otters and consequent overgrazing of kelp by sea urchins.

The present northern sea otter population of Amchitka Island is about sixty animals per square nautical mile. Sea otters have also inhabited the Rat Islands for twenty to thirty years. In the Near Islands, however, the once abundant sea otter was virtually exterminated by hunting. Since 1959, there have been scattered reports of sea otters in the Near Islands, and in 1975 more than 250 otters were counted at Attu. Northern sea otters are returning to their former range, and biologists are generally optimistic about the animals' future survival.

It is the southern sea otter that has been most seriously threatened in recent times, because of shooting by abalone fishermen and collisions with motor boats. At present the populations appear to be fluctuating between 800 to 1,500 animals, with most of these concentrated in the fifty-mile-long area that has been made into a state refuge.

Sea otters appear to be beneficial to the abalone, as they prey on sea urchins which destroy large areas of kelp beds which are crucial to the survival of the abalone, by providing them with shelter and food. The sea urchin problem has become so critical that divers are being employed to kill urchins as a poor substitute for the otter which can work energetically around the clock. Yet despite this, abalone fishermen continue to blame the sea otters for their own folly and greed and many have shot otters on sight. However, human predation on sea otters has sharply declined since several abalone fishermen were convicted of shooting some of the animals. Today incidences of deliberate killing by man are almost non-existent, and the southern sea otters can regularly be seen in Carmel Bay, off parts of the Monterey Peninsula.

A federal law now prohibits the owning of a sea otter pelt without a special permit. The animal is carefully studied and supervised. Although it has rebuilt its colonies off central California, western Alaska, and in the Commander and Kuril Islands, the sea otter still has reoccupied only about one fifth of its former range.

Unfortunately, there is little prospect of re-establishing the animal in the part of its former range that extends northward along the Pacific coast of the United States and Canada, unless oil pollution can be greatly reduced, or better, totally eliminated. Unlike most marine mammals, sea otters do not have a deposit of fat under the skin to protect them against the cold; they are wholly dependent on air entrapped in their fur. If the fur becomes polluted by oil, it quickly loses its insulating properties, and the animal may die from cold and exposure.

The California Department of Fish and Game wants to manage the southern sea otter, to contain it within certain boundaries and possibly establish a sub-population elsewhere. In all, there are now some 1,700 southern sea otters (according to a recent government aerial survey) along a 160-mile stretch of the central California coastline, from Santa Cruz to a point just south of Morro Bay, and the population is expanding steadily each year.

Undoubtedly, strict protective measures have been responsible for retrieving the sea otters from the brink of extinction, and the future of these enchanting animals hasn't looked brighter since biologists confirmed their reappearance forty years ago.

CHAPTER 12

BROWN PELICAN  *Pelecanus occidentalis*

The brown pelican is a large, dark grey-brown water bird with a wingspread of six and a half feet. Upon reaching adult age, the dusky-brown summer neck band, bordered with white, turns completely white for the winter season. Immature birds are grey-brown above and on the neck, with white underparts. This bird flies with its head hunched back on its shoulders and its large, pouched bill resting on its breast, and feeds by plunging head first into the water to capture fish, which form the mainstay of its diet.

Two distinct subspecies of brown pelican are recognized in North America: the California brown pelican *Pelecanus occidentalis californicus*, the larger race, occurs on the Pacific coast, from the state of Washington to Mexico, but nests solely on California's Channel Islands and the coastal islands of Lower California; and the eastern brown pelican *P.o. carolinensis*, which formerly bred in large numbers from North Carolina to the gulf coast of Texas and south to South America. Originally it was a common breeding bird in Louisiana but it was extirpated there, and was also more common on the coast of Texas and northwestern Mexico. Today, the eastern brown pelican in North America is in healthy numbers only in Florida.

Brown pelicans have declined drastically throughout most of their range. This has almost certainly been caused by the collapse of thin-shelled eggs and other impairments to reproductive success. Thin egg shells have been shown to be associated with excessive amounts of DDE (a breakdown product of DDT) in their fish food, the contents of pelican eggs, and in the tissues of the pelicans themselves. Dieldrin is also probably associated with this lack of reproductive success. Despite being pushed back by man's occupancy of so much of North America's coastal lands, the brown pelican held its own until the mid-1950s when its population collapsed from the use of chlorinated hydrocarbon pesticides. Fortunately, timely restrictions on the use of these poisons have promoted a slow comeback of brown pelicans and other fish-eating birds.

Prior to 1968 no one would have thought there to be any danger to the California brown pelican population. Then, in the late spring of that year, a team of biologists, headed by Dr. Daniel Anderson, found thousands of abandoned nests and very few birds in California's most northerly breeding area, Anacapa Island, sixty miles off the coast of Los Angeles. Out of 1,000 nests only four young birds had survived; the eggs shells were too thin – the weight of the adults on the nests had crushed them. In 1971 only seven young pelicans were produced in 600 nesting attempts on Anacapa Island. In that same year, however, researchers found the Sea of Cortez, apparently not polluted by DDT, to be swarming with many kinds of sea birds, including brown pelicans. A new colony was subsequently found on Coronado Island, off San Diego, where thirty-six brown pelican chicks were found in one day in one nesting colony.

Since 1972, which saw the use of DDT banned on this continent, brown pelican hatchings have been increasing. It is encouraging that in 1973, the U.S. Wildlife Management Institute stated that California brown pelicans had started on the road to recovery with the report that 305 young were hatched on Anacapa Island as compared to only one produced in 1970.

In 1974 over 1,000 chicks were found on Anacapa and Coronado Islands, and the California Department of Fish and Game and U.S. Fish and Wildlife biologists also found brown pelicans to be nesting on West Anacapa Island, the Channel Islands National Monument, and nearby on Santa Cruz Island. Similar reports of successful nestings on several islands off Mexico are encouraging signs that California brown pelicans are recovering from reproduction failure due to pesticide poisoning.

Unlike some species that protect their young from threats of danger, adult brown pelicans abandon their nests when intruders appear. An unattended nest leaves young chicks vulnerable to the heat of a blazing sun, which can kill them in minutes, and also to crows and gulls, which prey on pelican eggs. If older nestlings are approached, they may try to escape, usually falling to the ground or into the water. Once out of the nest the parent birds ignore them. Undoubtedly, the National Park Service's action in closing West Anacapa Island to the public during the nesting season has contributed to the increased nesting success.

Near the little town of Sebastian, midway down Florida's east coast, the huge flocks of eastern brown pelicans presented excellent targets in the 1900s for even the clumsiest marksmen. Here, on a three-acre island, where the pelicans nested, vacationers and plume hunters alike casually picked off the birds by the thousands. Not until 1903, when President Theodore Roosevelt, as part of the new National Wildlife Refuge System, set aside Pelican Island, Florida, as a "preserve and breeding ground for native birds," did the slaughter finally stop, and a man named Paul Kroegel was appointed to be the preserve's first federal game warden.

From that modest beginning seventy-five years ago, the National Wildlife Refuge System has grown into 385 havens, totalling over 30 million acres and sustaining almost every kind of wildlife in the United States. Currently, Pelican Island, now expanded to 756 acres, has a thriving population of eastern brown pelicans, as has South Carolina's 34,000 acre Cape Romaine National Wildlife Refuge.

Scientists believe Louisiana – where the brown pelican is the official state bird – once had the largest population of this species in the United States. According to wildlife writer Bill Thomas, old records indicate there once were at least 50,000 breeding pairs of these birds along the Louisiana coast. In 1933 ornithologist H.C.

Oberholzer recorded 2,300 eastern brown pelican nests alone on North Island in the Chandeleur group. But thirty years later less than 200 nesting pairs could be found in the same area. By 1961 the 4,550 pelicans, once known to nest on Mud Lumps at the Pass à Loutre, at the mouth of the Mississippi River, had completely disappeared, as had another colony on Belle Pass Island that had previously numbered 1,000 nests. By 1968 not a single brown pelican could be found along the Louisiana coast.

Likewise in Texas the eastern brown pelican population had almost disappeared. In the Lone Star State only four pelican nests could be found in 1967, while a year later there were two. The brown pelican had also become extirpated in Alabama and Mississippi, and had declined drastically in North and South Carolina. Only in Florida was the pelican holding its own and biologists were watching the populations there with concern. The eastern brown pelicans that once numbered in the millions could now be counted in the thousands, and species extinction became a real possibility.

Scientists and biologists were at first mystified at the pelican decline. "We thought it was due to a combination of factors," said Rockefeller Wildlife Refuge director, Ted Joanen. "We figured, for example, that the bad weather we had was making it difficult for the birds to catch fish and that this strain was just enough, in combination with the pesticides, to cause the die-off." It is now generally believed that the big die-offs were caused by pollutants flushed by heavy rains down the Mississippi River from farming areas further north. The same was largely true for the situation in Texas. Researchers concluded that the presence of DDE had upset the birds' calcium-producing metabolism, causing thin-shelled eggs too fragile to support the weight of a parent bird. Tests revealed high concentrations of DDT, DDD, DDE, dieldrin and endrin in the dead birds.

The fate of the eastern brown pelican was indeed in a precarious position in 1968, when a summit meeting was held at the Rockefeller Wildlife Refuge, with Sandy Sprunt, chief research director for the Audubon Society, acting as chairman. Also participating were top representatives from Louisiana and Texas, as well as from the U.S. Fish and Wildlife Service. The purpose of the meeting was to devise a program which would reverse the declining trends, and somehow bring about a resurgence in the eastern brown pelican population.

As a result of the summit conference, it was decided that Louisiana and Texas would both attempt to re-establish their eastern brown pelican populations by the transplanting method. The birds were to be taken from Florida, where pelican populations appeared to be stable. The first transplant was conducted that year with fifty pelican chicks from Florida's healthy population, numbering 6,000 breeding pairs. In 1971 the first nesting colony in ten years was reported in Louisiana, and for years after the brown pelican populations in Louisiana and Texas increased. The U.S. Fish and Wildlife personnel worked in co-operation with Louisiana Wildlife and Fisheries people to create the most favourable conditions for the pelicans and to afford them every protection.

All appeared to be going well until the spring of 1975, when disaster struck. Suddenly, within a two-month period, most of the birds disappeared, and wildlife officials were mystified. "Recent nestings had been very successful," said Allan Ensminger, chief of the Wildlife and Fisheries Commission Refuge Division. "There was no indication of trouble until that spring. We began to get reports of dead birds in May and early June. On June 10, one of our biologists made an aerial check on the number of free-flying browns – we do this every year and ordinarily spot 175 to 200 birds. In 1975 we could only locate about forty-five. By the end of June we knew we had real trouble, but we never have found all the dead birds. I'd say we located about twenty-five and that's all." The reason for this sudden disappearance was never discovered.

Plans now called for expanding the transplants to new sites along the Louisiana coast and in the summer of 1976, 765 Florida pelican chicks were moved to new areas around Barataria Bay near Grand Isle, Louisiana, and 221 young birds were fledged in Louisiana nests. During the summer of 1977, 100 eleven-week-old brown pelicans were again captured on Florida's tangled mangrove islands and put on a truck, bound for Barataria Bay. It has been more than ten years since efforts were begun to restore the eastern brown pelican to the Pelican State, where they once abounded.

Recent brown pelican nesting successes have improved dramatically both in California and in Louisiana, and aerial surveys conducted in Florida within recent years have sighted between six and seven thousand nests every year. Currently, the total number of eastern brown pelicans in that state is about 30,000. Happily, DDE levels in the eggs have declined quickly, thereby raising hopes for the success of further bird transplants to former nesting sites.

CHAPTER 13

FLORIDA MANATEE
Trichechus manatus latirostris

When Christopher Columbus travelled past the coast of Hispaniola (now the Dominican Republic and Haiti) on January 9, 1493, he observed what he believed to be three mermaids lift their heads above the water. The admiral recorded the event in his journal but added somewhat wistfully, "They are not so beautiful as they are painted; though to some extent they have the form of a human face." It was another nine years until Columbus encountered the mermaids again, this time at Azua on the south coast of the island, but by this time the legendary mermaids had been identified as large aquatic mammals known today as manatees or sea cows. Columbus' brief statement would appear to have been the first record of a manatee sighting.

Other sailors saw these animals with their rounded heads and arm-like flippers, as they returned with further strange stories of encounters with mermaids. With their bodies raised in a vertical position, revealing two nipples in the region of the breast, it is not altogether surprising that the sailors thought they had seen the legendary sea nymphs or sirens. The scientific name for the order – Sirenia – is of course based on this implausible story. According to Dr. Daniel S. Hartman, a wildlife biologist currently conducting

research studies on the manatee, "Any sailor who mistook a manatee for a siren must have been delirious. Still there is something lovable about the manatee. I have always felt that they are so ugly as to be beautiful."

The Spanish colonists who followed Columbus soon learned that the meat of the manatee made excellent eating. This animal, which somewhat resembles a whale, is actually more closely related to the elephant. However, it was classified as a fish by the Spanish church, therefore its meat was enjoyed on Fridays and other religious days.

At the time that Ponce de Leon rounded Florida, the Florida manatee *Trichechus manatus latirostris*, which is geographically isolated from its cousin, the West Indian manatee *T.m. manatus*, was commonly distributed throughout the coastal waters and lagoons from the Florida Keys to North Carolina, and was even found in Virginia, although these were probably stragglers. Currently, seldom seen north of Miami, they concentrate on the southern tip of Florida and range in sparse numbers westward to some parts of coastal Texas. The coastal fringe of Everglades National Park has a fairly large and well-protected population. They may also be found up the Suwanee River, and some have even been seen in the following Texas areas: Cow Bayou, near Sabine Lake, Capano Bay, Laguna Madre, and around the mouth of the Rio Grande. Two other manatee species are known to occur: the South American manatee *T. inunguis*, of the Amazon River system; and the West African manatee *T. senegalensis*, which occurs on the West African coast from Senegal to Angola.

Manatees, and their cousins the dugong *Dugong dugong*, are the only members of the order Sirenia, and are also the only large, herbivorous mammals living in shallow waters, both fresh and salt water. They have all been exploited by man in all parts of their range to the verge of extinction, especially in the tropics. Seminole Indians once hunted Florida manatees not only for their meat but for their hides and oil, and for a while, near the turn of the century, a rage for "sea beef steaks" almost succeeded in wiping out the animal.

The Florida manatee is a dull greyish to dark grey, large aquatic mammal with a rounded body and a small head. The animal's eyes are small and it has no external ears. Generally, manatees grow up to twelve feet or more in length and weigh about 1,200 pounds. Its forelimbs have evolved into flippers, and its body ends in a broad, horizontally flattened, rounded fluke. Manatees are shy, retiring, and humble creatures. They do not fight for territory or food, and are content to be left alone to munch plants. Their worst, if not their only, enemy is man.

Up until the present time, man has totally exterminated only one species of sea cow, but that was one of the most dramatic extinctions that man has brought about. The species in question was the Steller's sea cow *Hydrodamalis stelleri*, a coarse-skinned sirenian, twenty-five feet long, which occurred in the Bering Sea and on the Coast of Kamchatka, unlike other members of its order which dwell in tropical or subtropical climes. This largest of known sirenians was discovered by Georg Wilhelm Steller in 1741, during one of the Russian exploration voyages that led to the discovery of Alaska. Steller noted that these sea mammals lived in herds and fed together on kelp. When a sailor hooked one, the other animals tried to save it, circling the victim or jostling the boat; once, for two days, a male of the species continued to swim in close to a beach where its mate lay dead. Shortly after Steller's voyage the fate of the big, defenceless, and edible sea cow was sealed. By 1755 it had been hunted almost to extinction throughout its range, and finally in 1768, just twenty-seven years after its discovery, the last Steller's sea cow was seen.

The decline of other sea cows can in the main also be attributed to the same cause – overhunting for their meat. Manatee meat is much like beef, although it varies considerably in texture and colour, even within the carcass of a single animal. Besides that, the meat lends itself well to salting and smoking, and could be kept for some time by people who had no ice. Noel Vietmeyer, writing in the *Smithsonian* magazine, informs us that, "Hunting for profit takes a high toll and during a two-year period early in this century, more than 8,000 were slaughtered in Brazil, and in 1963, hundreds and probably thousands were slaughtered in Peru when uncommonly low levels in the Amazon headwaters made them vulnerable."

Although now legally protected in most countries they inhabit, their numbers have dwindled because enforcement of laws is impossible in the remote swamps, rivers, and estuaries where they are located. They are also caught unintentionally in fish nets where they tangle and drown. Although Florida manatees are protected within their range in the United States, the 1,000 or so native specimens are still in danger. Not only are they shot at, but they are often maimed by the propellers of big powerboats. Also contributing to their decline are the facts of increasing deprivation of territory by developers and the pollution of Florida waterways.

There are practical reasons for preserving the manatee. Water hyacinths and other aquatic weeds cover hundreds of thousands of acres of waterways in Florida and Louisiana – although they cover vastly greater areas in parts of the tropics. Indeed, the explosive growth of aquatic weeds threatens to become one of the world's greatest environmental problems; aquatic plants harbour mosquitoes, carriers of malaria and encephalitis, and can impose an oxygen-depleting load on the water.

Scientists at Florida Atlantic University believe they have found a way to use the manatee and at the same time save it from extinction. One adult manatee may eat a ton of aquatic vegetation a day. Since many estuarine rivers and canals in the warm climates of the world are now choked with water hyacinths introduced from the tropics, manatees could be a boon in clearing these channels for navigation. Whereas chemical and mechanical controls can eliminate the water hyacinths for one to three months, a hungry manatee uproots entire plants and prevents new growth for up to six to eight months. The only problem in Florida is that during the few cooler months the water temperature drops. The manatee is unfortunately vulnerable to the effects of cool temperatures, and many specimens have been known to have died of respiratory diseases and bronchial pneumonia when it has been unseasonably cold.

An abortive attempt was made in 1964 to use manatees to help clear Florida's choked waterways of water hyacinths, but seven of the eight animals involved in the project died, most of them from pneumonia induced by cold weather, though two of the manatees were known to have been maliciously killed. For as long as they could survive the manatees' weed-clearing feats were spectacular but the end results suggest that their usefulness is likely to be limited to the true tropics. A reminder of the manatee project is ever present at the Bio-Science Building at Florida Atlantic University; in a glass case is contained the mounted body of Claire, an eleven-foot manatee. Claire was one of the eight animals enlisted as "biological agents" in the 1964 attempt to eradicate the water hyacinths.

In March 1973 the National Research Council of Guyana asked the National Academy of Sciences in Washington, D.C. to meet and devise solutions to problems caused by aquatic weeds in Guyana. And, in February 1974, a further meeting of science councils from Guyana, international organizations, and researchers from eight countries, was held in Guyana to consider further the manatee's plight. The first steps are under way to establish an institute, a committee of scientists has been organized to direct the first phases, and the government of Guyana has generously offered to provide land and legal statutes to allow for research facilities.

There is no evidence of decline in the number of Florida manatees within the past decade; although no reliable estimates exist, at least 1,000 of these animals are believed to inhabit the state's coastal waters. Despite the fact that the manatee's range has been greatly reduced, the Florida manatee may actually be more abundant than is believed at present, due to the fact that it is one of the most difficult of all totally aquatic mammals to observe in the wild. The animal is granted full legal protection in Florida, especially in the Everglades National Park – the largest sanctuary for the manatee in the country – and at Chassahowitzka, J.N. "Ding" Darling, and Merritt Island National Wildlife Refuges.

Blair Irvine, wildlife biologist for the U.S. Department of the Interior, believes that "the manatee recovery story seems promising only in the United States where the animals have been protected since the turn of the century. In other countries the outlook is poor to uncertain because of continued human utilization."

CHAPTER 14

CALIFORNIA
CONDOR *Gymnogyps*
californianus

When a huge, black-feathered bird was found dead in a field in the California central valley in the spring of 1966, a commotion took place in wildlife circles. This discovery also touched off an intensive investigation by the state and federal governments. The object of all this concern was a California condor.

Investigators first ruled out shooting as the cause of death. They also decided that the bird had not been the target of a rock thrower, or a victim of a hit-and-run driver. They eliminated the possibility of poisoning from farm pesticides. Finally the verdict came: the bird had flown into a high tension power line. In Berkeley, a spokesman for the National Audubon Society lamented, "It's terrible, just terrible. The death of that bird makes us sick." The reason for all the anguish and concern was the fact that the California condor is one of the rarest birds in the world, with a total population probably not exceeding fifty individuals.

Adult condors are all dark brown or black, except for a triangle of white feathers on the underside of the wings. The head is bare orange. Together with its beady eyes, the bird conveys a sinister appearance which does nothing to improve its general image.

As a matter of fact, it is a harmless and timid bird and its

benefits as a scavenger cannot be overestimated. In addition, the condor is a much cleaner bird than is generally accredited; one of its favourite habits is to assemble on the bank of some secluded mountain pool and spend hours at a time bathing. Because of its heavy weight, the condor cannot take off directly from a flat surface but must run for several yards into the wind before launching itself into the air. So, when it alights on the ground to feed, it must have plenty of unobstructed space from which to take off again. When perching, it selects a dead limb on a tall tree or the edge of a cliff from which it can fly with ease. Although on land it is a thing of no great beauty, in flight the condor is poetry in motion. The bird soars motionless, on its outstretched wings for miles in the same position. By riding the up-draft it can travel about forty miles an hour at altitudes of up to three miles.

The California condor is one of the largest flying birds in the world, certainly the largest in North America, weighing up to twenty-five pounds, and with a wingspread approaching nine and a half feet from wing tip to wing tip. This huge bird has only one superior. It will give way when feeding to the golden eagle; otherwise the condor is sole monarch of the skies in the few areas in which it still exists.

Towards the end of the Pleistocene epoch, some 10,000 years ago, a huge ancestor of the condor *Teratornis merriami* flourished throughout the southern United States as far as Florida. Fossil remains indicate that it was a gigantic bird that must have sported a wingspan of about seventeen feet, but in all other aspects it very closely resembled our present-day bird.

In historic times, California condors were found from the Columbia River in Oregon, south to northern Baja California, and east to southwest Utah. Here they were seen soaring in their hundreds. At one time these great birds would fly to the coast to feed on the sea food thrown up on the shores. In fact, the first written account of this species in 1602, was made aboard ship by a Carmelite friar, who reported a mass of them feeding on the carcass of a beached whale on Monterey Bay. Skeletons of the birds have been found far inland with marine shellfish remains included as apparent food fare. But the California condor no longer journeys to the sea.

In 1769, Spanish explorers assisted at a ritual sacrifice of a condor at an Indian encampment; the Indians of the southwest revered the condor and called it "The Thunderbird." And the Lewis and Clark expedition reported sightings of the bird along the Columbia River in 1806. The great bird probably bred in nearly all of California's many mountain ranges, even as recently as a hundred years ago, although it vanished from Oregon no earlier than 1860.

Today, the heart of condor country is Los Padros National Forest, which extends along the mountainous California coast and encompasses 1,950,000 acres of California's wildest land. This area contains two special condor havens, the 1,200-acre Sisquoc sanctuary and the 53,000-acre Sespe sanctuary.

Little was known about the status of the condor until the National Audubon Society, with the aid of the University of California and the U.S. Forest Service, made two detailed studies, the second of which was financed by the National Geographic Society. The first study, made in the late 1940s, counted at least sixty condors, but by the time the second study was made in the early 1960s, the number had dropped to about forty.

When, in October 1965, a careful count was made over a two-day period by the California State Fish and Game Department, the U.S. Forest Service, the U.S. Bureau of Sport Fisheries and Wildlife, and the National Audubon Society, only thirty-eight condors were sighted. It became evident to all concerned that drastic measures had to be taken if this unique species was to be saved.

This prompted the California legislature to pass a law doubling the penalty for taking, killing or injuring a California condor. Anyone violating this law now receives a $1,000 fine or a year in jail or both. The National Audubon Society appointed a full-time warden; state game wardens were also on full alert in the protection of the birds, and the U.S. Forest Service stepped up patrols to keep the nesting and roosting areas in the Los Padros Wildlife Forest free from disturbances. The vicinity of the sanctuaries is strictly prohibited to all but three biologists who only make occasional visits. Visitors may enter the sanctuaries part way, but anyone found straying off the road without a permit can be prosecuted.

Hazards to the survival of the California condor include careless hunters, diseased carrion, power lines, malicious rock throwers, and pesticides. At one time, the main objective of several collectors was the obtaining of condor eggs. One egg was bought by a collector in 1909 for $300, while some collectors' catalogues have listed the trading price of the eggs of a condor at $500. It is unfortunate that most newspaper accounts have stated that condor eggs are extremely valuable. In the Los Angeles *Times* of May 14, 1939, a price of $750 each was publicized in an article entitled "Eggs $9,000 a dozen," and in the same newspaper of August 8, 1949, condor eggs are said to be worth $500 to $1,000 apiece. Obviously, this erroneous and deplorable publicity has tempted people to seek out condor eggs.

Mortalities resulting from all the aforementioned causes, however, have only been contributing factors in the decline of the condor population since European man reached the West Coast. The magnitude of the problem probably increased following the advent of the high-powered rifle in the 1890s, and continued only slightly abated until recently. Had it not been for protective measures during the years following 1925, the condor might already be extinct.

There may have been misguided reasons for killing condors. Farmers and ranchers believe, even today, that the condor kills livestock, particularly new-born lambs, calves, and fowl. Ironically, the condor is strictly a scavenger and it has never been known to attack a living mammal. Despite the bird's great size, the condor has the foot of a turkey and nails instead of talons. Yet, because many farmers are convinced that this bird is a threat to their livestock, condors have suffered from poisoned bait used to exterminate wolves and other predatory animals. In California, the wholesale destruction of the coyote and the ground squirrel was organized in this way; first with strychnine, later with thallium sulphate and finally with the even more virulent "compound 1080."

Once there was a more rational reason for killing condors. Their great quills were used by miners for carrying gold dust, as they could hold ten cubic centimeters when fitted with a wooden stopper; many hundreds of these birds were killed just for their quills. Undoubtedly, egg snatchers may have also put a heavy pressure on the bird. According to Sandford R. Wilbur, research biologist for the U.S. Fish and Wildlife Service, a minimum of 204 condors and fifty-four condor eggs are known to have been collected for scientific and hobby purposes, over half of them between 1881 and 1910.

The condor is in some ways its own worst enemy as it does not mate until it is six years old. The female produces only one egg every two years, and it is believed that the male takes only one mate during its lifetime. Compounding the problem is the condor's fear of people. During the crucial five-month nesting period, when the infant condor is gathering strength for its first flight, the parents will abandon their young if humans come too close. Blasting a mile away can be equally unsettling, and as road-building crews and mining teams have moved into the area, the condors have disappeared.

Despite the fact that in 1963, the condor was designated by the state of California as a protected species, two condors were known to have been shot the very same year, and another one the year after. Although legal protection goes back over a hundred years, only one man is reported to have been punished for killing one of these rare birds. In 1908 a man was fined $50 for killing a California condor. The state government has taken a good many steps to safeguard the bird, but a substantial part of the public has been unwilling to co-operate.

As recently as September 1976, a California condor was found shot by hunters in southern California. According to naturalist John Borneman, the bird had suffered for at least two weeks with a broken wing and infection; it weighed less than twelve pounds, about half its normal weight. "The condor will probably live," reported Borneman, "but it is doubtful its wing can be saved or that it can be returned to the wild where less than 50 of its kind survive."

Since 1968 only about fourteen new condors have been added to the population. Sandy Wilbur maintains that to keep the numbers stable approximately thirty-two new birds would be needed. As an indication of this production deficit, condor numbers have declined from approximately sixty in 1965 to fifty or less in 1976. Some condors must now be reaching advanced ages and could die at any time, the total number to decrease even more.

In 1969, the California Condor Recovery Team was formed,

with Sandy Wilbur leading a group of biologists selected by the U.S. Fish and Wildlife Service. The team consists of representatives from federal and state wildlife agencies, and from the National Audubon Society. Among the items included in the recovery plan are proposals for land acquisition, for reducing human disturbance in nesting areas, for supplementing the condor's food supply, and for further research in an effort to improve general understanding of the bird's requirements. Much of the plan has now been put into effect, and it has been a valuable exercise in developing support for an endangered species. However, despite much good work undertaken by the recovery team, the key to increased production in the wild has not been found.

Thus, the major priority is that a captive breeding program be initiated, whereby condors are taken into captivity with the purpose of increasing their breeding rate and returning them to the wild at a later date. It should be possible under those conditions to hatch the eggs in incubators and raise the young away from the parent birds, allowing the adults to start nesting anew. The captive young would be released back into the wild to supplement the free-living population.

Regarding their release back into the wild, California condors should be easier to establish than some other species because they do not need to be taught to hunt and kill their food. Their dependence on carrion makes it easy to provide them with adequate food in desired locations while the birds are becoming used to their free existence. Sandy Wilbur says:

> To be fair, it has to be said that it is not certain that a program of captive propagation will help the California condor survive. At this point, we don't know. However, it is my opinion based on seven years' working with these birds that they will probably not make a comeback without some supplementing of their production. The desire to save the condor is great, however, and the current level of co-operation among state, federal and private organizations is high, perhaps as high as for conservation of any other species of wildlife. If the population still has the capacity of sustaining itself, then we can be at least cautiously optimistic that the shadows of soaring condors will still flow over California's ridges and canyons for yet a few more years."

CHAPTER 15

EASTERN TIMBER WOLF
Canis lupus lycaon

No mammal on the endangered list has inspired more debate than the eastern timber wolf, which prowls a narrow bio-political terrain. Many of the facts concerning the status of this animal have been confusing and contradictory. The timber wolf population in Minnesota's Superior National Forest, according to a *New York Times* writer, "could well be double the official 1971 state estimate of 750 to 800," and he called for a recommendation for wolf numbers to be curtailed in their last stronghold in the United States. Around the same time, the state of Michigan filed suit against a clothing store in Lansing to stop the sale of coats trimmed with wolf fur, as Attorney General Frank Kelley warned that the animal "is on the very edge of extinction."

This subspecies is only one of twenty-four recognized races of the timber or grey wolf *Canis lupus* inhabiting North America, four of which are already considered extinct, while the Rocky Mountain wolf *C.1. irremotus* and the Mexican wolf *C.1. baileyi* share endangered species status with the eastern timber wolf.

A lack of understanding of the true nature of the wolf and the vital role that it plays in the scheme of things has caused it to be pushed towards extinction over most of its range. Although

eastern Canada may harbour as many eastern timber wolves as it ever did, south of the border, only two or three states still boast small remnant populations that survive in wilderness areas close to the Canadian border.

Michigan repealed its wolf bounty in 1961, and has perhaps forty wolves left. These wolves are confined to Isle Royale National Park in Lake Superior, which also supports a herd of about 600 moose. Wolves first appeared on the island about 1949, coming across the frozen lake from Ontario. Since that time, their numbers have remained remarkably stationary. Before the arrival of the wolves Isle Royale suffered an overpopulation of moose in the 1930s, with the resultant overbrowsing and deterioration of the island's vegetation.

The status of the eastern timber wolf in Wisconsin is uncertain; there may possibly be a resident population of about 100.

Minnesota has the most eastern timber wolves of all – estimates range between 1,000 and 1,200 – living in its forested northern counties, occupying about one third of the state. These wolves are mainly represented in the Superior National Forest. The wolf bounty in Minnesota was repealed in 1965, after vehement outcries from many farmers and sportsmen. The hunters claimed that the big dogs were a menace to the deer population, despite evidence that Minnesota has one of the healthiest deer herds anywhere, and that deer hunters usually have their greatest success in wolf country.

It would appear that outright protection of the wolf in Minnesota is politically impossible. In 1964 the state legislature passed a bill which would extend bounty payments on wolves. Governor Karl Rolvaag vetoed the bill, giving wolves, for a few years at least, a slightly better chance of survival. He was defeated for re-election the following year, and many people called his "pro-wolf" stand a factor in his defeat.

At present the government is under great pressure from anti-wolf forces to have the wolf bounty reinstated. There is a good chance that they will succeed. However, the Minnesota Conservation Federation, the state division of the Izaak Walton League, and the Fund for Animals, are working for the protection of timber wolves in the state. It is encouraging that in the last stand the eastern timber wolf is finally receiving some support.

This animal formerly inhabited Canada and the United States, east of the Mississippi River, except for Mississippi, Alabama, and Florida, and is replaced in northern Quebec and mainland Newfoundland by the Labrador wolf *C.1. labradorius.* The cause of its demise has been human settlement of extensive wilderness areas, which had two devastating effects on the animal. First, it usurped a great deal of habitat from the deer, moose, beaver, and other large mammals which constitute the wolf's prey. Second, it brought the wolf into direct confrontation with man because of its tendency to prey on livestock. Thus, deliberate and indiscriminate extermination of the wolf was carried out by farmers and ranchers with the support of state and federal governments. Minnesota was paying a bounty on wolves up to 1965, and Ontario was even meting out wolf bounties as recently as 1972.

The bounty on the eastern timber wolf has since been removed but, in the heyday of the system, even park wardens could collect the bounty for shooting wolves. As recently as 1958 it was considered part of the game warden's job to shoot wolves in Ontario's Algonquin Provincial Park. Today, in Algonquin Park, the practice of wolf shooting has given way to the far more enjoyable pastime of "wolf howling." During the latter part of August several thousand visitors gather at Algonquin Park's Lake Opeongo to hear wolves howl in response to human imitations of their calls. "It's a mind-blowing, hair-raising sound," says a Hamilton, Ontario, wolf buff and a supporter of the Ontario Wolf Defenders' League. "It's impossible to describe or forget. I just thank God they're still out there in the woods."

Slowly we are coming to recognize the place of the wolf and other predators in the natural order of things. By its very existence, a wolf ensures the continuance of the species it preys upon. Almost invariably, it kills the weak, old, and the infirm, leaving the fittest to perpetuate a healthy prey population. Nevertheless, throughout history wolves have been held in bad repute; in song and in folklore, wolves have been ferocious killers that were to be dreaded at all times. Early settlers feared for their lives when the mournful cry of the wolf was heard echoing across the empty land.

Early naturalists were equally uninformed; an old natural history book, which I have had since I was a small boy, entitled simply *Untamed*, gives this defamatory account of the wolf's character:

They are skulking cowards in summer, when food is plentiful – grey shadows, slinking from tree to tree, and attacking only creatures smaller and weaker than themselves. But the famine times of winter often drive them to a madness of hunger, and they are then a terror to all – Man himself is not safe from them. The leader of the pack gives tongue – the Wolves' "Tally-ho!" – a truly frightful sound to the ears of whatever poor beast they are bent on pulling down.

Naturalists rated high among those who perpetuated the "big bad wolf" myth.

Studies made in recent years show that the danger of attacks by wolves were very much exaggerated. It is also realized that there is not one authenticated case of a timber wolf killing a human being in the history of settlement in North America. The exception would be when a wolf becomes rabid, but the incidence of this disease among wolves is rare. It is particularly interesting to note that wildlife workers who tag wolves do not find it necessary to drug the animals during the tagging operations. Wolves are not the ferocious killers that they are believed to be. James W. Curran, editor of the *Sault Daily Star* of Ontario, in 1925, posted a reward of $100 for any person in Algoma County (where wolves were numerous) who could prove that a wolf had attacked a human being. The reward was never claimed, although more than ninety reports were investigated.

Bounty payments for eastern timber wolves were made in the United States for over 300 years, the first being made in Massachusetts in 1630. In that year, the Massachusetts Bay Colony established the first bounty system in America by offering one penny for every wolf shot. Many were able to earn a living from such bounties, giving some indication of the numbers of wolves that must have been shot during this period.

It took over 200 years to exterminate the timber wolves in the United States east of the Mississippi River; by 1850 they had disappeared from all but a few areas, and by 1900 they had been

131

exterminated throughout the East, except for the northern parts of Wisconsin, Minnesota, and upper Michigan.

A wolf bounty was one of the first acts passed by the Upper Canada legislature in 1793. The first recorded figures show that in 1947, Ontario paid out $59,275. In 1970, it paid $69,996 for the heads of 1,255 eastern timber wolves, 2,047 coyotes and 43 pups. However, according to the late Frank A. Walden, director of the wildlife branch of the Ontario Ministry of Natural Resources in 1973, the Ontario eastern timber wolf population remained at a stable 10,000 to 12,000.

West of the Mississippi other subspecies of wolves persisted in considerable numbers until the 1930s. It is likely that the mountains would have provided a refuge for these animals had not grazing become such big business on national forests and other public lands. The grazing interest would not tolerate predation of livestock and in 1915 Congress appropriated funds for the control of animals injurious to agriculture. It was the death knell for the large predators in the western United States.

Because of the animal's imperilled status in the United States, the Eastern Timber Wolf Recovery Team was established with a committee of eight biologists representing the states of Michigan, Wisconsin, and Minnesota. Also, the U.S. Forest Service and the National Park Service were appointed by the U.S. Fish and Wildlife Service. The purpose of the recovery team is to devise a master plan for the recovery of the eastern timber wolf throughout as much of its former range in the United States as is biologically feasible.

According to Dr. David Mech, wildlife research biologist for the U.S. Fish and Wildlife Service, many Minnesotans believe a wolf bounty is needed again – especially those people living in the 31,000 square miles of wolf range. They cite as their reasons a declining population of deer and the loss of domestic livestock to wolves. The introduction, in the summer of 1976, of a federal bill to provide $500,000 in livestock damage payments to Minnesota farmers during a five-year period, indicates the severity of the problem. The Eastern Timber Wolf Recovery Plan would, therefore, appear to be an imperative measure.

Currently, the recovery plan is in draft form. It has undergone review by many expert wolf biologists, and by state and federal officials, and is being considered for approval by the U.S. Fish and Wildlife Service.

David Mech feels it significant that the "recovery team" has recommended by seven to one that the Minnesota eastern timber wolf population be upgraded from the endangered status to "threatened." Although from a national viewpoint the eastern timber wolf is restricted to about 5 per cent of its former range in the United States, the species is not endangered within Minnesota. At present the Endangered Species Act (1973) makes it illegal for anyone to kill an eastern timber wolf in the United States. But the recovery team believes that for the sake of successful, long-range conservation of the wolf in Minnesota, some individuals will have to be sacrificed.

Prior to the formation of the recovery team, some state and federal biologists in 1974 trapped four eastern timber wolves in Minnesota. They measured them and fitted them with radio collars, so that their movements could be monitored, and released them in Michigan's Upper Peninsula. This was part of a reintroduction program to endeavour to restock wolves in some of their former territories. Other possible reintroduction sites were also considered: the Maine woods, New York's Adirondacks, and the Great Smoky Mountains of North Carolina and Tennessee.

This reintroduction program did not, however, sit well with the hunters of Michigan, for within eight months three of the wolves had been shot, and the fourth had been run down by an automobile. The eastern timber wolf was again extinct in the Upper Peninsula.

"It may be," says David Mech, "that in fifty years from now, despite the recommendations of the Eastern Timber Wolf Recovery Team, the animal will survive in the United States only in Isle Royale National Park, Voyageurs National Park, and the Superior National Forest of Minnesota." Fortunately, the eastern timber wolf still thrives in healthy numbers in parts of eastern Canada, so that its future survival on this continent is assured, at least for the time being.

CHAPTER 16

WHOOPING CRANE *Grus americana*

In the winter of 1974-75, only forty-nine whooping cranes existed in their natural wild state. Native only to North America, these majestic birds have declined to their present population level from an estimated 1,500 to 2,000 in the nineteenth century.

The whooping crane, which had ranged across the marshes of the prairies of this continent, retreated before the white man's settlement until its breeding grounds in the United States had all been abandoned. Its period of decline continued through the 1930s until only one migratory flock remained in the wild, wintering in a single marsh on the south coast of Texas. Despite the fact that they never made particularly good eating, hundreds were slaughtered for sport. By 1941 their numbers had reached an all-time low of fifteen.

In 1937 the United States government, in an effort to protect the species from extinction, purchased this area as a migratory refuge, since named Aransas National Wildlife Refuge. At the time when the only nesting area was discovered in Wood Buffalo National Park, Northwest Territories, on June 30, 1954, there were only twenty-one wild whooping cranes in existence. While the isolated nesting grounds provided protection, the far northern location

meant a short nesting season. Furthermore, the crane's migration route was long and dangerous: 2,600 miles from Wood Buffalo to Aransas, made twice a year.

For a species whose numbers had been diminished to less than two dozen, and which has a very low reproductive rate, the prospects for a natural resurgence seemed slim. Whooping cranes have always been known to reproduce poorly. The two eggs laid usually hatch, but one of the two chicks almost always dies, due to sibling rivalry and competition for food. Therefore, nearly half of the whooping crane nesting effort is wasted owing to loss of eggs.

With that thought in mind, Canadian and U.S. Wildlife Services embarked on an operation to collect whooping crane eggs from the wild for use in a captive propagation program. That involved transporting eggs from whooping crane nests in Wood Buffalo National Park to the Patuxent Wildlife Research Center in Laurel, Maryland, for artificial incubation, hatching, and raising. The objective was to establish a breeding flock that would eventually produce enough birds to restock the wild population.

Beginning in 1967, Ernest Kuyt, and other Canadian Wildlife Service biologists, entered the whooping cranes' breeding areas and took six eggs, one from each nest. As a result, the parent birds could devote themselves to the solitary remaining egg and, when it hatched, to the single chick. The chick, therefore, would receive twice as much parental care and protection as it would have under normal conditions, giving it an increased chance of survival. Ten more eggs were picked up in the following year and another ten in 1969, with the last egg pick-up being made in 1974. Since the experiment began more young cranes arrived in Aransas from the flocks hatched in those years when whooper eggs were picked up.

Meanwhile, the eggs taken by the wildlife biologists were rushed by jet plane to the Patuxent Center to be hatched under artificial conditions. Of the fifty eggs collected in 1967, 1968, 1969, 1971, and 1974, eighteen have been raised to date, making the hatching success rate higher than it would have been in the wild.

On April 18, 1975, an egg was laid by one of the whooping cranes at Patuxent, the first egg laid in the captive flock that has resulted from airlifting second eggs from clutches laid on the natural breeding grounds. This is the first time that a whooping crane hatched and reared in captivity has in turn laid an egg. Unfortunately, the chick died some days after hatching.

The same year co-operation between the Canadian Wildlife Service and the U.S. Fish and Wildlife Service, the University of Idaho and the Idaho Department of Fish and Game, resulted in a unique experiment which may further strengthen the survival prospects of the severely endangered whooping crane.

An egg transplant program involving greater sandhill cranes (a distinct but similar species) as foster parents, hatching and rearing whooping crane chicks, was initiated at Grays Lake National Wildlife Refuge in Idaho. Dr. Rod Drewien's six-year study of a flock of greater sandhill cranes led the U.S. Fish and Wildlife Service to believe the sandhill cranes could hatch the extra eggs from Canada and raise the whoopers as foster chicks – teaching them sandhill crane survival methods as well as the sandhill migration route. If successful, the project would establish a second population of whooping cranes in the wild, outside the migratory range of the present flock.

The male whooping crane reaches a height of up to five feet with a wingspread of seven feet, making it the tallest bird in North America, while sandhill cranes are a little smaller. Whooping cranes are whiter and have a more massive bill than the sandhills; they are also distinguished by black-tipped wings. The two species have many behavioural similarities. Both mate for life, and require a territory of some thirty to forty acres in which to nest and raise their young. Whooping cranes always nest in aquatic areas, while sandhills usually do as well. Both return to the same nesting grounds each spring, to within one and a half acres of the same spot. If they lose a nesting area through the intervention of man neither will seek another location.

Both males and females of both species share the incubation of the eggs of which only two are normally laid each year, and the eggs of the two species are almost identical. On average the whooper's egg is only one millimetre in size larger and although the colouring is very slightly different this is not readily discernible to the sandhill crane.

The U.S. Fish and Wildlife Service carefully selected Grays Lake greater sandhill cranes for the project, based on bird-banding data and observations of marked birds. Cranes that showed a strong tendency to spend the winter at Bosque del Apache National Wildlife Refuge in New Mexico were chosen because both Bosque del Apache and Grays Lake can provide a high degree of safety for the birds. The migratory route between the two areas is about 850 miles long, only a third as long as that travelled by the cranes migrating from Wood Buffalo to Aransas.

Grays Lake National Wildlife Refuge in Soda Springs, Idaho, is one of the largest nesting grounds for sandhill cranes, measuring nine miles by four miles, and surrounded by fields of grain. Banding of the sandhill cranes and the study of migratory routes has been conducted at Grays Lake for many years by the Idaho Cooperative Wildlife Research Unit. After carefully considering the project's chances of success, the various agencies finally took the plunge in 1975. They gambled fourteen of the thirty-one whooping crane eggs laid that spring in Wood Buffalo National Park.

Nine of the fourteen eggs transferred eventually hatched, and of these nine, six whooping cranes lived to begin the fall migration to New Mexico. The six whooping crane chicks left with their foster parents between October 2 and 22, 1975. Their route south took them through Monte Vista Refuge in Colorado, then to Bosque del Apache. Four chicks were located. Two were found at Bosque del Apache, one at Helen State Game Refuge, and one at a nearby farm. The other two whoopers were never seen again and are believed to have perished on the journey south.

The immature whooping cranes integrated well with the sandhills at the wintering grounds. At first some sandhills attempted to attack the whiter whooper cranes. But the foster parents defended their chicks when this happened and such incidents became infrequent.

Strict precautions were taken to protect the immature birds from hunters and predators throughout the winter. Since winter hunting was permitted in some places near Bosque del Apache, each time one of the whooping cranes took flight a horn was sounded warning hunters to hold their fire. This was in addition to many notices that were put up saying that the whooping cranes were in the area and describing their appearance. No harm came to the four young birds during their first winter.

The return flight of the sandhill crane flocks began in early February 1976. All four of the young whoopers were seen at Monte Vista National Wildlife Refuge with their foster parents, resting on the return flight to Grays Lake. But the sandhill cranes rejected the juvenile birds before reaching Grays Lake. This rejection of their young is a natural process with the sandhills, which enables them to start a new nesting cycle. It had been hoped that the return migration would have been completed before the young birds suffered the normal rejection by their foster parents.

In late May 1976 the four whooping crane chicks were still at Monte Vista, apparently with no intention of flying on to Grays Lake. They had to adjust to being on their own through the spring and summer. Assuming this happens successfully, wildlife biologists hope that by the time the cranes mature sexually in four or five years, they will return to Grays Lake for breeding purposes.

In early December 1976, three whooping crane chicks from the 1976 breeding project were in Bosque del Apache with the foster sandhill parents. It is expected that in due course they will select whooping crane mates, rather than sandhills. In addition to the plumage and size difference, the two species' calls and ritual dances are different. A female of one species would very likely be unresponsive to courting by a male of the other species.

The fostering experiment will be under constant evaluation and is planned to continue until 1981. The project is dependent upon the nesting success of the main whooping crane flock at Wood Buffalo National Park. In May 1976 a further fifteen whooping crane eggs were taken to Grays Lake and placed in sandhill crane nests; unfortunately, three of these were destroyed by coyotes in June.

Thus far the experimental cross-fostering program has been a qualified success. Hopes are high that the long-range experiment will succeed in establishing a second flock of whooping cranes. Although the future for the whooping cranes has never looked rosier, the only certainty is the need for continued intervention by man.

An Audubon volunteer sighting network is currently being organized by National Audubon research director, Sandy Sprunt, and David Blankinship, a wildlife biologist in Texas, in co-operation with the U.S. Fish and Wildlife Service. The object of this exercise is to monitor the main whooping crane population, and document each rest stop, particularly in the northern Great Plains where federal irrigation and drainage projects threaten to dry up vital wetlands.

The volunteers, armed with binoculars, will fan out across the prairies and sloughs from mid-March through early June, keeping records of each whooper sighting. They will do the same during the cranes' return flight in the fall. This data will be used to persuade the federal government to preserve critically needed rest stops.

The flock of whooping cranes at the Aransas National Wildlife Refuge during the winter of 1976-77 numbered sixty-nine, which means that all fifty-seven of the 1975-76 adults returned, along with twelve new young. And in the sandhill crane fostering program, five of the "fostered" whooping cranes are known to be still alive after the second year of the experiment. During the fall of 1976 more young cranes survived to the migration state than in any year since 1938.

According to the National Audubon Society, 1976 was called a "banner year" for the whooping cranes, but it seems the whoopers' flag has only begun to unfurl. As of midsummer 1977 there were 120 whooping cranes in the wild and in captivity, the largest count since records were first kept in the 1930s.

CHAPTER 17

SAN JOAQUIN KIT FOX
Vulpes macrotis mutica

Kit foxes are small, desert-dwelling foxes of greyish or buff colouration with black-tipped, bushy tails, and proportionately very large ears. Acute hearing serves these animals better than smell in the dry desert air, which tends to evaporate scents. During the day these shy mammals usually laze in dens they have built in soft soil, occasionally among the roots of a tree or cactus. At night, they hunt lizards, insects, rabbits, and rodents – especially kangaroo rats – by running them down or digging them out of the ground. Because of their nocturnal habits, kit foxes are rarely seen, even in areas where they are not uncommon.

These animals are also extremely fleet of foot and over a distance of one hundred yards the kit fox is one of the fastest animals. This attribute has been responsible for one of its common names "swift fox." The name "kit fox" refers to the animal's small size; it is only about two thirds the size of a red fox *Vulpes vulpes*, or a little bigger than a house cat. It averages only a weight of four to five pounds.

Kit foxes are divided into various races, all of which are rapidly decreasing in numbers and range. Since the opening of the West these animals have generally become common victims of the

poison bait put out for rodents and coyotes. Attractive and trusting, the kit fox has been unable to prosper in the face of adversity, as have other wild dogs such as the red fox and the coyote *Canis latrans*.

Formerly kit foxes ranged in open, sandy areas from central Alberta and Saskatchewan way down south into Mexico. Untold numbers were trapped and snared as settlers moved into their habitat and much of the necessary cover was either irrevocably altered or destroyed. This was the pattern on both sides of the border until only widely scattered pairs or individuals remained. Some races have become restricted solely to small, isolated areas, while one of these, the southern California kit fox *Vulpes macrotis macrotis*, is already extinct. This race formerly ranged in southern California chiefly in the Lower Sonoran life zone. It was extensively killed for its fur and large numbers were trapped; but it was also killed by poison during campaigns against coyotes. The last southern California kit fox was trapped in the San Jacinto plain in 1903.

The International Union for the Conservation of Nature and Natural Resources has also listed the northern kit fox *Vulpes velox hebes* in its red data books of endangered species. This subspecies was formerly common throughout the great central plains of Canada and adjacent northern United States. It is now probably extinct in Canada as a result of trapping, poisoning, and hunting, but has not entirely vanished from the United States, where increasing numbers have been sighted in recent years.

Dr. Thomas Childs, a Canadian federal government veterinarian, reported on the intelligence and agility of the kit fox as a participant in a sport popular in parts of southern Alberta a little over half a century ago – the hunting of coyotes by horsemen with dogs:

> During such hunts it was quite common to rouse a Kit Fox and of course the dogs would take off after the fox. Dogs which could, without too much difficulty, overhaul and destroy a coyote, could outrun the Kit Fox. However, catching the little rascal was definitely not an easy matter. When the fox realized the dogs were overhauling him, he would reduce speed just enough

to encourage the dogs to even greater efforts; then when it appeared he would surely be picked up, the fox would swing his tail assembly (brush) hard aport or starboard, leap sideways as lightly as a puff of thistledown, reverse his course, and float away at top speed. The dogs – strong, weighty animals, travelling at top speed – would invariably overrun the point at which the fox reversed course, and after braking to a stop, and reversing course to renew the chase, would find the fox had opened a very substantial lead. That sort of performance usually continued until either the dogs were exhausted and gave up the chase, or the fox had managed to disappear from view.

If there was a barbed wire fence in the vicinity – such fences usually consisted of three strands of barbed wire strung on posts, with the lower strand of wire 16 or 18 inches from the ground – little vulpes astuta would invariably lead the pursuing dogs directly to the fence, and pass under the lower strand of wire at top speed; the pursuing dogs, having their eyes on the fox and nothing else, would usually strike the lower wire at top speed – frequently with disastrous results to the dogs, and terminating the chase very abruptly. The writer has seen this form of sulpine strategy in operation on more than one occasion.

In the California desert country lifeless zones are uncommon. The vegetation may be relatively abundant, chiefly composed of creosote bushes and cacti, and such deserts may even serve as a refuge for certain animals. To these semi-arid regions some animals have adapted themselves by evolving certain specialized characteristics, such as the San Joaquin kit fox *Vulpes macrotis mutica*, the race which, because of its decline, currently requires the most attention.

The San Joaquin kit fox formerly inhabited the drier parts of the San Joaquin Valley in California – from Tracy, south. Today it is found only from the Tehachapi Mountain foothills, surrounding the southern end of the San Joaquin Valley, north along the foothills of western San Joaquin Valley, to Byron, Contra Costa County, and on the eastern edge of the valley, north to Viscalia.

The reasons for the animal's decline have been primarily the reduction of the rough, dry, valley land habitat to highly irrigated

146

agricultural areas. Also, the foxes appear to have been susceptible to certain rodenticides which may have been used in the area. The most recent threat, however, has come from the irresponsible use of "game calls" to attract them to be shot or illegally trapped.

On the basis of research studies conducted on behalf of this animal in recent years a San Joaquin Kit Fox Recovery Plan has been developed and implemented to assure the animal's continued survival. A decline in the kit fox population was first noted by federal and state wildlife agencies, and its plight called to the attention of the California Department of Fish and Game and the U.S. Fish and Wildlife Service in the 1950s and 1960s.

In 1965 the California Fish and Game Commission responded by declaring both the San Joaquin and the desert kit fox *V. m. arsipus* as protected fur-bearers. And in the following year, the Secretary of the Interior designated the San Joaquin kit fox to the status of endangered.

A life history study of the animal was subsequently undertaken that year by Stephen Morrell, wildlife biologist for the California Department of Fish and Game, in co-operation with the U.S. Fish and Wildlife Service. The results of the study pointed to the possibility that rodent control of the Beechey ground squirrel *Spermophilus beecheyi*, using compound 1080 (Sodium monofluoroacetate), might be having an adverse effect on the kit fox through secondary poisoning. In 1971, on the basis of the department's findings, the California Fish and Game Commission declared the animal a rare species under the California Endangered Species Act (1970), which prohibits the taking or possessing of rare and endangered species without a proper permit.

In 1972 the California Fish and Game Commission closed portions of Kern, San Luis Obispo, Fresno, Kings, and Monterey Counties to all-night hunting and fur-bearer trapping after it was determined that illegal shooting of the San Joaquin kit fox was taking a significant toll.

In 1973 the California Department of Fish and Game and the California Department of Food and Agriculture monitored the effect of an aerial application of compound 1080-treated bait set out for ground squirrels. Five adult kit foxes in the area were fitted with radio telemetry collars and their movements carefully noted

147

before and after the application of the poisoned bait. Nine additional kit foxes were noted within half a mile of compound-1080-treated areas, but no impact on these animals from the ground squirrel bait was observed during the program.

These surveys resulted in a decision by the California Departments of Fish and Game, and Food and Agriculture, and the U.S. Fish and Wildlife Service, to jointly fund a one-year study, during 1974-75, to determine the distribution, abundance, and status of the San Joaquin kit fox.

As a result of the survey, the kit fox population, taken from the total kit fox area, was estimated at a minimum of around 5,000 and a maximum of 15,000 individuals, with a mean figure of 10,000.

The San Joaquin kit fox recovery team has recommended areas for critical habitat determination by the Secretary of the Interior, and the California Department of Fish and Game is translocating foxes under immediate threat of habitat loss. In the opinion of Howard R. Leach, Non-game Wildlife Co-ordinator for the department, the San Joaquin kit fox is not threatened with extinction because of the extensive foothill habitat area and the relative stability of land use in this portion of the animal's range. Everything possible is being done to preserve the native habitat of the ecosystem in which the rare and local San Joaquin kit fox has evolved.

CHAPTER 18

ALEUTIAN CANADA GOOSE

Branta canadensis leucopareia

The Aleutian Canada goose, a very small subspecies of the familiar Canada goose, with a darker plumage and a shorter neck, once bred from the central Kuril Islands to the Islands of Four Mountains in the eastern Aleutian Islands, and wintered in northern Japan and in California. These birds provided food for Aleuts, explorers, and sealers, especially during the summer when the birds moulted and were unable to fly. The subspecies is nearly indistinguishable in the field from the slightly larger Taverner's Canada goose *Branta canadensis taverneri,* or the slightly smaller cackling Canada goose *B.c. minima.* Aleutian Canada geese vary in breast colour and the immature birds have only small neck rings, as do some individuals of the other races.

Arctic foxes, introduced to most of the island homes of the Aleutian Canada goose for fur-bearing purposes, eliminated the birds on all except Buldir Island, a volcanic island in the western Aleutians, which was too isolated and too poor a harbour for the fox farmers to use. Rats were accidentally introduced, and also became ready predators on eggs and young chicks. It is on Buldir Island that the last established 200 breeding pairs of Aleutian Canada geese are known to survive.

The Russians instituted the practice of introducing foxes in the Aleutians and Kurils in the early 1800s and by the 1890s only a few Aleutian Canada geese were to be found where they were formerly plentiful. The last birds were recorded on these islands in 1914 when fur farming began to expand from a very low level in the Aleutians.

Between 1910 and 1930 nearly every island was stocked with Arctic foxes, and in the mid-1930s Dr. Olaus J. Murie was sent to the Aleutian Islands to investigate the effects of foxes on the nesting birds. Dr. Murie found geese on only a few of the Western Aleutian Islands where Dr. Austin Clark had previously found geese "breeding by the thousands" in the 1880s. The Second World War and reduced fur prices brought fur farming to an end in the Aleutian Islands; but the foxes remained.

In the late 1940s Robert D. Jones, Jr., the first resident manager of the Aleutian Islands National Wildlife Refuge, took the first action on behalf of the geese. During the next twenty years Jones and his assistants eliminated all foxes from Amchitka Island, and significantly reduced the population on Agattu Island. Jones was determined that a remnant breeding population still remained on Buldir Island in 1962. He captured goslings there and used them to start a captive flock to reintroduce on fox-free islands to help reestablish the population.

The first release of captive birds, involving seventy-five three-year-old geese, was made in 1971 at Amchitka. A few of the birds were killed by bald eagles *Haliaaetus leucocephalus*, but most apparently left the island shortly after their release. Unfortunately, the birds were never seen again. In May 1974, forty-one Aleutian Canada geese were released on Agattu Island, but of the four pairs that nested only two were successful. Then nine geese were taken from Buldir Island, during their summer moult, and brought to Agattu with the objective that they would lead the other geese during the winter migration. The birds migrated as planned on September 4, but all are believed to have met with disaster. Two of the birds were shot in northern California that winter and one more was sighted. None returned the following year to Agattu Island. It would appear that captive breeding of these geese is only successful when released specimens are able to establish themselves and breed in a wild environment.

In 1974 the Director of the U.S. Fish and Wildlife Service appointed a recovery team of six biologists to develop and implement a plan designed to restore the Aleutian Canada goose (by then declared officially as an endangered species) to a safer population level. The team consists of G. Vernon Byrd (the recovery team leader), Paul F. Springer, Philip Lehenbauer and Ray Erickson of the U.S. Fish and Wildlife Service, Frank Kozlik of the California Department of Fish and Game, and Daniel Timm of the Alaska Department of Fish and Game.

The first step in the recovery program involved eliminating the introduced Arctic foxes. In the past, the deadly compound 1080 and strychnine were able to be used because no native mammals occurred on the islands where the operation was being conducted. The baits were kept small in an attempt to prevent their detection by birds such as bald eagles, ravens *Corvus corax*, and glaucus-winged gulls *Larus glaucenscens*. The poisoning campaigns did not appear to have any noticeable effect on the gull populations, although the bald eagle and raven populations on Amchitka Island were reduced, at least temporarily. G. Vernon Byrd and Paul F. Springer, on behalf of the recovery team, feel that if fifty breeding pairs of these rare geese can be successfully reintroduced at two stations other than Buldir the race could possibly be upgraded from "endangered" to the less precarious status of "threatened." Further successful re-establishment at a third station should be sufficient to remove the bird from the list entirely.

The three stations selected for fox removal operations and subsequent goose reintroductions are isolated areas, in order to reduce the possible danger incurred by local disasters such as earthquakes and tidal waves. They are Agattu Island together with nearby Nizki and Alaid Islands, Amchitka Island, and Kanaga Island. The first selected site was Agattu Island, so chosen because it had supposedly been rendered fox-free. In addition, according to available literature it may have originally had the greatest population of Aleutian Canada geese of any of the islands. Nizki and Alaid Islands, just north of Agattu, were included in this same restoration area. Amchitka Island was chosen as the next desirable island since it was fox-free and the geese had formerly bred there. Kanaga Island, the third island chosen, required no fox reduction work but had also formerly been a breeding area for the geese.

In 1974 and 1975 Arctic foxes were hunted on Nizki and Alaid Islands, and a total of fifty-four foxes were taken at Agattu in the two years. The biologists estimate that between ten and twenty of the foxes remain. At Nizki and Alaid Islands, 130 foxes were taken in 1975, leaving behind an estimated fifteen to forty animals. The purpose of this fox reduction operation is an attempt to keep their populations low until chemical toxicants or M-44 cartridges may be considered. If approved, these methods would prove more effective and lead to complete fox eradication.

The second major part of the program is to produce the geese in captivity for prospective release into the wild. The original eighteen goslings, taken on Buldir Island in 1963, were held at Monte Vista National Wildlife Refuge in Colorado until 1966, when eight of the birds were sent to the Patuxent Wildlife Research Centre at Laurel, Maryland. An additional twenty-one goslings, taken at Buldir in 1972, and twenty in 1975, were also sent to Patuxent.

All together, over 325 Aleutian Canada geese were produced from 1966 to 1975, with geese taken from the wild for first generation birds being used as breeders. Pairs of Aleutian Canada geese have also been farmed out to carefully selected game breeders at various locations in the United States, Canada, and England. The ultimate goal is to produce up to 200 goslings every year. In order to accomplish this objective, a second production centre is to be established, and additional stock will be procured from Buldir Island to expand the breeding flock. In this way the desired production capacity may be reached by 1980.

Since Canada geese are popular game birds in western North America, it is important to discover their greatest population areas if the Aleutian race is to be protected and their numbers restored more quickly. Potential observers along the west coast of North America and the east coast of Asia have been notified about banded birds and told to watch out for them. In addition, arrangements were made for a student investigator to locate and study the geese on their migration and on their wintering grounds.

In the fall of 1975 an unsuccessful search for the geese was made on Vancouver Island and in Washington State and Oregon. However, up to 200 Aleutian Canada geese frequented Castle Rock, on the northern California coast, between late October and mid-November. A banded bird was shot east of the Sacramento Valley on November 11, and a mixed flock of 230 Aleutian and cackling geese was observed in the same locality during the latter part of that month. Eight other banded birds were reported as having been shot from November 1975 through January 1976 in Yolo, Contra Costa, Merced, and Imperial Counties in California. Also, a flock of forty probable Aleutian Canada geese was observed from late November 1975 to early February 1976 at the Grizzly Island Wildlife Area in Solano County. On January 10, 1976, the birds reappeared at Castle Rock, and thereafter their numbers increased. An estimated peak number of about 900 individuals were observed from late March to mid-April 1976.

As can be seen, the overall success of the recovery program depends largely on an integrated effort. Fortunately, there has been much excellent support and co-operation from federal and state governments and from private individuals. With continued co-operation one can be optimistic about achieving the recovery team's goal of restoring the Aleutian Canada goose to its original, non-endangered, non-threatened status.

CHAPTER 19

COLUMBIAN WHITE-TAILED DEER *Odocoileus virginianus leucurus*

KEY DEER *Odocoileus virginianus clavium*

White-tailed deer are one of the most popular game animals in North America, being found throughout the continent from southern Canada all the way south to northern South America, except for much of the Pacific coastal areas and the Great Basin. They are inhabitants of deciduous and mixed woodlands, showing a preference for river bottomland and stream sides.

This species is the familiar deer of eastern North America, where in most areas it is more abundant now than in colonial times. It is one of the most graceful and dainty of deer, with a long, slender neck, narrow face, and beautiful, baleful eyes. The white-tailed deer may reach a height of three and a half feet at the shoulder, and an extra large buck may weigh in at 350 pounds. The animal ranges in colour from some shade of reddish-brown in summer to blue-grey in winter, with some variations in between.

The Columbian white-tailed deer is the most northwestern of the thirty-one recognized subspecies of white-tails and has the most limited range. It is isolated from others of its species by geography and by its special habitat requirements. This rare subspecies, which once ranged west of the Cascade Mountains through the Willamette and Umpqua Valleys of Oregon, and

along the lower Columbia River, north to Puget Sound, has been reduced to a few hundred animals in the lower part of its range.

Today, the only place where this rare animal is certain to exist is along the lower Columbia River, near Cathlamet in Washington. According to field representative Raymond "Sandy" Davis, another herd of white-tailed deer exists in the region of the Umpqua River near Roseburg in southern Oregon, and may well be this subspecies, but this has not as yet been scientifically documented.

When Lewis and Clark recorded the first observation of the Columbian white-tailed deer during their explorations in 1806, the animal was abundant. However, when settlers followed and cleared the trees and brush from the valuable agricultural land along the river bottoms, the deer gradually dwindled and retreated to smaller and smaller isolated areas.

By 1900 agricultural development and logging had destroyed almost all the original habitat. As recently as 1934, S.G. Jewett, a prominent northwestern zoologist, declared that this subspecies was probably extinct, except for one small herd near Roseburg.

Then in 1939, after following reports of the existence of deer on the south side of the Columbia River, a local game warden found a recently shed antler on Puget Sound, which could only have come from a white-tailed buck. Meanwhile, farmers and fishermen testified that the deer was well-known and hunted along with black-tailed deer from the adjacent forested hills. Two local biologists, Victor Scheffer and Walter Dalquest, collected several of these animals, together with skulls and antlers, and shipped them to the Smithsonian Institution in Washington, D.C. They were subsequently confirmed as being Columbian white-tailed deer.

Unfortunately, at that time – and for many years after – much of the crucial riverside woodland was still being eliminated to make way for livestock pasture. Local farmers resented the deer's grazing on clover and grasses intended for their domestic animals, not to mention their feeding in gardens and on young fruit trees. As the habitat shrank, hunting increased, especially as during the Depression people couldn't afford to pass up easy venison. Unfortunately, the Oregon Wildlife Commission did not acknowledge the existence of the white-tailed deer, and the state of Washington made no distinction in its hunting regulations between white-tailed and black-tailed deer, the typical deer along most of the Pacific coast.

The fact that the deer could adapt to livestock pastures, if suitable patches of brush cover were nearby, was encouraging, but as the pastures expanded large areas were stripped of all cover. There was no way that the deer could adapt to these modified conditions and they disappeared from that area. Perhaps 150 Columbian white-tailed deer survived on Puget Island, but Deer Island, where Lewis and Clark originally found the animals, was devoid of deer.

In 1940 Victor Scheffer assessed the Columbian white-tailed deer population to be between 400 and 700 individuals. They had endured so long only because of the area's comparative remoteness and absence of competition from black-tailed deer. But without the establishment of inviolate sanctuaries, the long-range prospect of their survival was bleak in the face of agricultural encroachment.

Despite the imperilled state of these animals no concerted effort was made on their behalf for a quarter of a century, and they were legally hunted until 1968. However, law enforcement in the intervening period has been good, and farmers owning most of the habitat have been sympathetic to the deer, so that hunting is not likely to become a major factor contributing to their extinction. In 1970 and 1971 the states of Washington and Oregon closed the area to deer hunting along the Columbia River in the known Columbian white-tailed deer habitat.

The U.S. Fish and Wildlife Service began a land purchase program in 1972 to acquire suitable habitat for the deer in its two native states. In that year, the Columbian Deer National Wildlife Refuge was established in Douglas County in Oregon. The 5,200-acre refuge consists of river bottoms into which the Columbia River descends. Most of the moist land is devoted to grazing cattle and is divided into small, poorly drained pastures. Straddling the states of Washington and Oregon, the refuge includes Hunting and Price Islands, and a strip of the mainland near Cathlamet, all in Washington, and Tenasillahe in Oregon.

In addition to protecting the 300 or more of the estimated 400

Columbian white-tailed deer, the refuge is also part of the overall Columbia River wintering area for many species of waterfowl on the Pacific flyway that may congregate there in large numbers, depending on weather and habitat conditions.

The U.S. Fish and Wildlife Service feels it can manage with the available land, but a continuing effort is being made to provide protection for the deer known to exist outside the refuge, where land clearance and illegal hunting are still real threats. These deer include perhaps fifty Columbian white-tailed deer on Puget Island, another small herd of ten or so northwest of the mainland section of the refuge, and an additional thirty-five animals near Clifton in Oregon.

Currently, state hunting regulations permit the shooting of black-tailed deer across the road from the refuge boundary, a situation which has caused some problems. A few Columbian white-tails have also been shot by hunters who were unable, or unwilling, to distinguish between the two species. However, according to law, a hunter can be held accountable – ignorance notwithstanding – for violation of the Endangered Species Act (1973).

The Columbian white-tailed deer, unlike other races of white-tails, is primarily a grazer. There is a little spring browsing, but browsed plants make up only one per cent of the animal's total diet. This preference for grazing has helped focus efforts to maintain a favourable environment for this specialized animal.

Following guidelines laid down by the Endangered Species Act, a Columbian White-Tailed Deer Recovery Team has been established and consists of the refuge manager and biologists from Oregon State University, the two state game agencies, and the U.S. Fish and Wildlife Service. Studies are currently under way to better define the habitat requirements of the Columbian white-tailed deer. Their interaction with cattle, regarding grazing and haying, will be evaluated through the animal's response to these activities. Some of the deer are marked with plastic collars to facilitate study of their movements and their social interaction, so as to determine why the deer are restricted to such a limited habitat. Such information could be most helpful in the possible relocation of some of the animals.

With much-needed federal funding, and continued support of

the local people, the Columbian white-tailed deer population should retain a permanent foothold in part of its original range on the Pacific coast.

The Key deer, another endangered white-tailed deer, is the most famous land mammal of the Florida Keys. It can easily be distinguished from other white-tails by its very small size, paler colour and very small antlers. It stands less than two and a half feet at the shoulder and rarely weighs more than eighty pounds, approximately half the weight of a typical white-tailed deer.

Even before historic times, the Key deer was confined to the small islands of the Florida Keys. Here, the animal swam from island to island in an environment of coral reefs, salt-water marshes, and tropical hammocks. In recent years it has been eliminated from several of the Keys on which it formerly existed. A combination of habitat destruction, wanton hunting, with the aid of dogs and spotlights, real estate development, and seasonal hurricanes, brought this diminutive deer close to extinction.

Strangely enough motor accidents were also and are a major cause of death; even now, nine or ten deer are struck and killed by cars every year, about a third of the annual loss from all causes. It has been suggested that cigarette butts play a part in the accidental deaths. These diminutive deer apparently find tobacco irresistible and come regularly to the highway to look for butts tossed from passing cars. Like most wild animals, they have not yet learned to fear the automobile. Their small broken bodies are a familiar sight along the Key West Highway.

Shortly after the end of the Second World War it became apparent that another wildlife catastrophe was about to occur, this time in Florida. That state had already seen the near end of the egrets, the decimation of its alligators and crocodiles, the slow decline of the manatee, and the near extinction of the Key deer. A survey conducted around 1949 revealed that the little Key deer was estimated to number no more than twenty-five to thirty individuals, existing solely on the chain islands running southward from Big Pine Key to Boca Chica, seven miles from Key West, Florida. Conservationists everywhere were deeply concerned.

In 1951, through the joint efforts of the National Audubon

Society, the Boone and Crockett Club, the National Wildlife federation, and other groups, a game warden was hired to patrol the principal Key deer areas in order to protect the animals. With the establishment of the Key Deer National Wildlife Refuge on Big Pine Key in 1953, legal protection and effective propaganda helped restore the population of the deer. The refuge extends to 6,745 acres and includes the greater part of the animals' habitat. Of this total, 834 acres are federally owned; the government holds the remainder on lease.

By the early 1960s the Key deer population had risen to about 300, showing further evidence of the resilience of deer, when adequately protected. Currently, the total Key deer population, now occupying eighteen islands, stands at about 600. With protection of its habitat its survival seems assured.

Although the refuge in the Florida Keys is well patrolled, some natives have poached and shot an occasional deer. However, a tenfold increase in the Key deer population in a decade is evidence that most people living in or visiting the area have helped, and the Key deer has since been removed from the International Union for the Conservation of Nature's list of endangered species.

The Key deer is a living demonstration that a species can respond well to sensible conservation measures. Very often it is possible to avert an impending wildlife tragedy if the citizens of a land react swiftly and surely and in good faith.

CHAPTER 20

PEREGRINE FALCON *Falco peregrinus*

Without doubt there is nothing to equal the speed and grace of the peregrine falcon, a bird that has been prized by man for over 3,000 years. The Egyptians made golden statues of this bird and European kings and noblemen paid a fortune, even by today's standards, for a champion that could swoop down at 175 miles an hour and kill its prey with a knockout blow of its clenched foot.

The peregrine falcon has long been a creature of myth – its name means "pilgrim hawk" or "wanderer" – and has also been a victim of human exploitation. Falconers traditionally regarded it as second in value only to the gyrfalcon of the far North and it may have been the first in terms of numbers used.

Once common and widespread throughout Canada and much of the United States, the peregrine falcon has been declining drastically as a wild bird. The reason for this decline has undoubtedly been due to pesticide poisons, in particular DDE, the breakdown product of DDT, which are contained in the tissues of the birds on which it feeds. The cumulative effect of the poison appears to affect the calcium-producing elements in the female birds' bodies so that their eggs are formed with shells that are too thin to

withstand the wear and tear of incubation. In some cases there are no shells at all and the embryos quickly dehydrate.

Peregrine populations have survived centuries of depredations by game keepers, falconers and egg collectors. Beginning thirty years ago this graceful species disappeared abruptly from some regions and declined rapidly in others.

There are three recognized subspecies of peregrine falcons native to North America. Two of these, the American peregrine falcon *Falco peregrinus anatum* and the Arctic form *F.p. tundrius*, are officially regarded as endangered species. The American race, virtually extinct in the eastern half of the continent, rapidly disappeared in the 1950s and disappeared altogether in the 1960s, an early victim of egg shell thinning. The third subspecies, Peal's peregrine falcon *F.p. pealei*, is non-migratory in its habits and, consequently, is far less exposed to DDT than the other races.

Prior to 1950 small populations of peregrine falcons existed in the eastern United States and Canada, where they commonly occupied the ledges of skyscrapers and other tall buildings in the larger cities. There was a famous pair of peregrines that nested on a ledge of New York's St. Regis Hotel.

Perhaps Canada's most famous peregrine falcons were those that nested for a period of seventeen years, from 1936 to 1952, on the Sun Life Building of Montreal in the centre of the city. In 1951, some thousand or so bird-watchers observed the peregrines when the American Ornithological Society held its annual convention in Montreal. The society passed a vote of commendation for Sun Life's solicitude for these now-famous birds. The birds hatched their usual clutch, as they did again in 1952. But in 1953, the falcons did not return. Although they appeared to be in excellent health the birds must, in fact, have been suffering from the early effects of pesticide poisoning. One of the earliest accounts of aberrant behaviour of these Sun Life birds was given by the late G. Harper Hall as early as 1949. Between 1948 and 1952 many eggs disappeared; one embryo died in the shell and one chick died without apparent cause and Mr. Hall was mystified. The peregrine falcons have long been gone from that building.

Likewise, most eggs laid by peregrine falcons in Britain after 1946 were found to be thin-shelled. The cause of the thin shells has now been clearly established; it is due to the ingestion of sublethal amounts of pesticides, such as DDT and dieldrin, which became increasingly widespread in the years following the Second World War.

As far back as 1937 it was evident that the golden eagle, Britain's top bird of prey, was not raising broods of young in its eyries in the Scottish Highlands. The number of nests producing young fell from 72 per cent over the period from 1937 to 1960 to 29 per cent in 1961 to 1963. It was argued that the sheep dip used each year after dieldrin had been added to the vats remained as a residue in carrion that is the principal source of food for the eagles of the sheep-raising district of Western Ross. It is not difficult to prove where the danger lay. The dip formula was changed in 1966 and when the known eagle eyries were examined in 1968 the figures for breeding success rose from forty-six young per pair of adults to eighty-four. The eggs examined showed a significant reduction in dieldrin content.

Already the downward trend in the number of certain raptor species in the eastern United States has stopped since the 1972 ban on DDT, as these species have begun to breed more successfully. The peregrine falcon, however, seems not to have so far responded. Nowhere in North America have peregrine populations started to recover their numbers since the almost total reduction of DDT usage.

In 1970 a two-nation team of United States and Canadian investigating biologists checked 237 known peregrine falcon eyries, covering fifteen regions in Canada and Alaska. The empty nests they found revealed that poisons had spread northward. In southern Canada only four pairs were found in eighty-two eyries, while in the Arctic tundra fifty-three eyries yielded thirty-one pairs.

In 1975 a further large-scale survey of breeding populations of peregrine falcons was made throughout the known range of this bird in North America and Greenland. This program continued and extended the surveys begun in 1970, and is scheduled to be repeated at five-year intervals. The results of the survey show that almost all North American populations have declined further in numbers since 1970. Peal's peregrines are the only major population that has remained largely stable in recent years. Estimates placed the total population in the Queen Charlotte and Aleutian Islands at over 475 pairs.

The most significant development of the last seven years has been the successful breeding of peregrine falcons in captivity; not just a few birds, but on a scale sufficient for release and reintroduction into the wild. This can be attributed to Tom J. Cade, Professor of Ornithology, and his colleagues at Cornell University in Ithaca, New York, Richard Fyfe, and other wildlife biologists of the Canadian Wildlife Service at Edmonton, Alberta, and to other dedicated workers scattered over North America and Europe. Through their efforts more than a hundred fledgling peregrines have now been produced in North America, and an additional fifty in Europe.

The Canadian Wildlife Service's peregrine-raising program was begun in 1970. In that year, twelve immature peregrine falcons were taken into captivity at the service's facility at Wainwright, near Edmonton, to provide the nucleus for the captive breeding program. Additional birds have since been added. Species other than peregrines have also been accepted as experimental birds, such as prairie falcons, gyrfalcons, and Richardson's merlins.

The first success in the project came in 1971, with the captive breeding of prairie falcons, followed by successful natural breeding of peregrines, gyrfalcons and Richardson's merlins. Peregrine falcons from these captive breeding programs have been subsequently reintroduced into the wild. The most successful technique used to date has been "fostering," or placing captive-bred eggs or young under wild parents of the same species. Experiments were first carried out with captive prairie falcons. Most were hatched and all of the young were fledged by the foster-parent birds. This successful breeding of prairie falcons was subsequently extended to peregrine falcons in 1974 and 1975.

Another technique was used known as "double-clutching" which involves taking the first clutch of eggs and thereby forcing the pair to lay again. In 1974 clutches of eggs were taken from two wild pairs of peregrine falcons and three of five fertile eggs were hatched. The young were then raised in captivity until they were about three weeks old and then given back to the original parents.

The birds, in the interim had laid and hatched another three or four fertile eggs. The newly-hatched young were then all placed in one of the nests while their older (by three weeks) brothers and sisters were placed in the second nest. All of these young birds were then fledged successfully by the adults.

Since 1973 the Cornell University peregrine breeding project, under the guidance of its founder and director Tom Cade, has released most of their captive-raised peregrine falcons into the wild. Methods of releasing captive-bred birds have been the main stumbling block of many such projects. In the past large, solitary migratory birds rarely, if ever, have been successfully re-established. The peregrine falcon releases at five eastern sites were designed to exploit the falconry technique called "hacking," to introduce parentless fledglings into the wild.

Release sites were selected for an abundance of natural prey and for the security they afforded against both human and natural enemies. Two natural sites were chosen, a historic peregrine nesting cliff near Ithaca, and another in the Shawangunk Mountains near New Paltz, New York. An additional chosen site was a man-made structure, a seventy-five-foot-high gun tower on Carroll Island in Chesapeake Bay, off the coast of Maryland, from which poison gas shells were once shot at the ground below. This proved to be the most successful as well as the most dramatic site. Ironically, these nerve gas tests that made the island uninhabitable for humans in the 1960s spared it DDT sprayings.

In 1975 four fledgling peregrine falcons, a male and three females, were brought to Carroll Island, where they were placed inside a wooden box-like eyrie, where bars kept the young falcons confined until their flight feathers grew. Then tiny radio transmitters were attached to their legs so they could be tracked. The juvenile birds flew soon after the bars were removed and began to chase and strike at passing wild birds. To further encourage them to hunt and kill domestic pigeons were released at the foot of the tower, a falconry training technique, and the peregrines quickly grasped the idea.

In all, sixteen young peregrine falcons bred at Cornell University were released at five sites in the eastern United States in 1975. Twelve of them survived their first winter and were supplemented by two dozen more released in 1976. Three young peregrines, the first in many years, were successfully fledged in New Jersey the same year, making them the first peregrines known to have been reared in the United States east of the Mississippi for the last fifteen years.

There are good indications that attempts to re-establish the peregrine falcon in areas where it is nearly or wholly absent may succeed. A major question has been whether captive-bred peregrines would remain close or return to their release sites two or three years later to breed. Biologist Stanley Temple of the University of Wisconsin, who conducted the 1975 release as a research associate of Cornell University, says this 40 per cent first-year survival equals that for wild-born peregrines. The birds' return to their release sites is the more remarkable because all peregrines released by the Cornell team in 1975 are progeny of Arctic peregrines, and it had been feared that they would migrate deep into South America in winter, as Arctic peregrines do, and would then overfly the lower forty-eight states.

Also encouraging was the large number of peregrine falcon chicks hatched and returned to the wild in 1976. Cornell University put out forty-one young peregrines, and Richard Fyfe and his Canadian Wildlife Service colleagues put out thirty-eight. Most of the birds were gradually weaned back to the wild from release sites. Also, four Cornell chicks put into nests of wild peregrines survive in the West, and fifteen Canadian young were similarly handled to bolster an existing but threatened wild breeding population.

A novel Canadian move has also been to release an additional thirteen peregrine falcons inside cities – Edmonton, Hull, Ottawa, and Montreal. According to Richard Fyfe, cities provide adequate food supplies – pigeons – that carry low levels of pesticide residues. Also, peregrine falcons are easier to observe in a city than in a wild area. Thus far, Canadian city residents have accepted the raptors.

Wilderness areas have not been neglected in research, however. In September 1977, four young falcons bred at Alberta's captive-breeding facilities were released in Algonquin Provincial Park in Ontario. They appear to be adjusting but it is a little too early to

169

foretell the outcome. According to Ontario Resources Minister Frank Miller, "Peregrines, like humans, can be very selective when choosing a mate." Now all the birds have to do is survive their enemies, the weather, the winter flight south, and the new chemicals man has developed since the ban on DDT.

The sport of falconry is forbidden in much of North America. Where it is allowed, falconers must have basic knowledge of raptor identification and fulfil various other requirements connected with the welfare of their birds. The new federal regulations arise out of the United States' treaty with Mexico, which extends federal protection to virtually all birds used in falconry.

Peregrine falcon biologists in the United States and Canada have demonstrated a remarkable success at what was once thought to be only a dream. As Tom Cade wrote recently: "You climb a mountain, so I am told, because it is there to be climbed. You attempt to breed falcons in captivity and restore them to the wild because it is a challenge that most people consider impossible."

CHAPTER 21

KIRTLAND'S WARBLER *Dendroica kirtlandii*

Many wildlife communities and habitats have been destroyed by rampaging forest fires. Ironically, the Kirtland's warbler actually benefits from forest fires, which permit the reversion of burned-over land to jack pine growth which it appears to require in order to survive. Heat from the fire is needed to open jack pine cones to release the seed, while preparing the ground for the germination of that seed.

It has been said that, ounce for ounce, the Kirtland's warbler has drawn more official interest and created more controversy than any other songbird in history. This species nests only at the base of young jack pines *Pinus banksiana*, and will not nest in any area where the pines are more than eighteen feet in height. Therefore it must constantly shift its territory. The nest is built on the ground and is well hidden in the undergrowth. Four or five eggs are laid in June and incubation by the female bird lasts two weeks. Theoretically, should it fail to adapt to a more specialized habitat, and should fire be entirely controlled within its range, the Kirtland's warbler would become extinct.

This handsome, bright yellow-breasted warbler, with a striped, blue-grey back and black-streaked sides, breeds solely in jack pine

thickets in a small area of northern lower Michigan, principally in Crawford, Oscoda, and Roscommon Counties. Owing to its restricted range and exacting nesting requirements, the Kirtland's warbler has always been a rare species. It is one of the rarest, certainly the most local of the wood warblers, with a maximum population of 1,000 individuals.

It was not until 1851, that the Kirtland's warbler was discovered as a species, when a male bird was taken on May 13 on the outskirts of Cleveland, Ohio, and sent to the Smithsonian Institution. The bird was given to Dr. Jared P. Kirtland, a noted Ohio naturalist, and father-in-law of the founder, Charles Pease. Kirtland in turn gave the bird to the great ornithologist Spencer Fullerton Baird, who named the bird after his old friend in the following year.

The first Kirtland's warbler ever taken was a specimen collected by Samuel Cabot in October 1841 on board ship between Abaco in the Bahamas and Cuba, while on his way to collect birds on the Yucatan Peninsula. The specimen lay unnoticed in his collection until long after it had been truly discovered.

The winter range of the Kirtland's warbler was found when a specimen was collected on Andros Island in the Bahamas on January 9, 1879. At least seventy-one more specimens were subsequently taken during the winter on Andros and other Bahama Islands, but only five more spring migrants – four from Ohio and one from southern Michigan – were collected before the turn of the century. The collectors who frequented the Bahama Islands found the species to be fairly abundant between 1880 and 1900. Alas, this is no longer true. Logging and burning operations increased the area of jack pine during the period 1880 to 1910, making more nesting habitat for the Kirtland's warbler. Consequently, a short-lived upsurge may have occurred at that time when optimum habitat was probably at its greatest in hundreds of years, allowing collectors to take a number of specimens on the Bahama wintering grounds.

The discovery of the nesting area was made by an experienced ornithologist who heard an unfamiliar bird singing among nearby jack pines. He shot a specimen and took it to the University of Michigan's curator of birds, Norman A. Woods, for identification. Subsequently, Woods searched for and discovered the very first Kirtland's warbler nest in July of 1903. It was located in Oscoda County, about one half-mile east of the Crawford County line and a mile north of the AuSable River. All subsequent Kirtland's warbler nests have been found within sixty miles of this spot.

The sense of excitement expressed by Norman Woods in his discovery is well contained in his report:

I have just found a pair of Kirtland's warblers and, as I write, the female is three feet away, fluttering her wings, and seems very anxious. I am near a small heap of brush and logs and maybe the nest is here. . . . As I go around on my hands and knees, I see she keeps very near. . . . Down the jack pine he went. . . . No bird, no nest! I watched a few minutes longer and saw the female in the low jack pines. I watched her and she seemed very uneasy (having just been flushed from the nest). I began looking carefully on the ground, as I had made up my mind it would be found there. Suddenly I saw the nest! . . . In the nest were two young birds a few days old and, as luck would have it, one beautiful egg . . . pinkish-white, thinly sprinkled with chocolate brown spots gathered in a wreath at the larger end.

After Woods' discovery, other researchers continued to pursue the mysteries surrounding the Kirtland's warbler. For example, why were they so few in number? In 1930, Josselyn Van Tyne, curator of birds at the University of Michigan's Museum of Zoology, set out to find some of the answers. Between 1930 and 1956 he spent much of his time both in the nesting area and on the Bahamian wintering grounds, but died in 1957 without having published his findings.

Until 1951 no one knew even approximately how many Kirtland's warblers existed, because no one had visited more than a fraction of all the nesting sites. Then, on the hundredth anniversary of the species' discovery, a group was organized by Harold Mayfield of the Michigan Audubon Society to seek out every nesting location and count all the singing males. The number of singing males is a good measure of colony size since Kirtland's warbler males are almost always monogamous. The count was repeated in 1961. These two censuses, taken ten years apart, showed no essential change, suggesting that the population was holding steady at about 500 pairs, despite an ominously low production of fledglings.

In 1963, the U.S. Forest Service established the 4,010-acre Kirtland's Warbler Management Area in Michigan's Huron National Forest, where a plan for controlled burning over a larger area was brought into being. Twelve 320-acre sectors were set aside for this purpose. The date of the first burn was May 1964, and by September two hundred seedlings per acre had germinated. The success of this operation induced the Forest Service to burn twelve sectors approximately every five years.

In the census of 1971, however, the count of singing males had sunk to 201, a decrease of 60 per cent in ten years. The reasons for this decline were not fully understood. There were many hypotheses to account for this sharp reduction in Kirtland's warblers, not the least plausible of which was the unremitting pressure of the brown-headed cowbird *Molothrus ater*, a species that habitually lays its eggs in the nests of many small bird species and has a distinct predilection for the nest of the Kirtland's warbler. The warbler is an "accepter" species and tends to care for the cowbird eggs and young which have replaced its own.

The brown-headed cowbird developed this unusual behaviour early in its history, leaving the host birds with the chore of hatching the cowbird eggs and rearing their young in place of their own. Through the evolutionary process the cowbird has lost all nest building and tending behavioural traits and has become a nesting parasite on many species.

A newly-hatched cowbird is larger than the warbler chick and gets more than its share of the food brought to the nest by the adult warblers. With one cowbird in a warbler's nest, one to three of the warbler chicks may survive. If two cowbird eggs are laid and hatched, however, none of the warbler chicks will survive. The young warblers that hatch soon die since they cannot compete for food with the larger and more avaricious cowbird chick.

Harold Mayfield feels that the cowbird expanded its range from the grasslands of the central continent with the clearing of the eastern forests for agriculture, and reached the Kirtland's warbler's nesting ground for the first time during the 1870s. It found the warbler to be a perfect host, convenient and tolerant. Mayfield's studies show that during the 1940s and 1950s, the Kirtland's warblers lost 36 per cent of the fledglings they would have produced if there had been no cowbirds in the region. This is a severe, perhaps unprecedented, pressure from one predatory agent on an entire species of birds year after year.

In an effort to reverse the decline of this species, the U.S. Forest Service, in co-operation with the Michigan Department of Natural Resources and the Michigan Audubon Society, launched a cowbird control project in 1972. Trapping and shooting were the methods employed, with trapping proving more effective; 2,200 cowbirds were taken in traps during the 1972 season. A small increase in the warbler nesting population in 1973 of 216 pairs may have been a result of the cowbird control program.

Cowbird control continued and in 1974, 4,000 cowbirds were removed from the Kirtland's warblers' habitat. However, despite the removal of the cowbirds, the warbler population that year dropped to 167 singing males or 534 breeding adults. Since all seemed well on the Michigan nesting area, the recovery team pondered on the possibility either of changes on the Kirtland's warbler's wintering ground in the Bahamas that could be a threat to the species, or on their migratory routes. The reason for the decline was puzzling and never discovered. For a small increase followed in 1975 from 167 to 179 singing males, which gave a glimmer of hope that the decline in the Kirtland's warbler's numbers was being reversed.

The Michigan Audubon Society in 1976 reported a further increase from the 1975 census, an 11 per cent gain to 199 singing males compared to 179. This means that currently there is a breeding population of 398 Kirtland's warblers, plus an undetermined number of non-nesting birds.

The small, localized Kirtland's warbler population points to the significance of recent sightings of this species in Ontario. In September 1977, the Kirtland's warbler was added to the Ontario list of endangered species on the strength of over a dozen sightings recorded from that province since 1900. The most recent sightings occurred in June and July of 1977 in jack pine stands near Pembroke, close to the Quebec border, where a male bird was photographed, mist-netted and banded. Ontario Ministry of Natural Resources biologists are trying to determine whether a small breeding population of Kirtland's warblers survives in any of Ontario's jack pine regions.

In the meantime, a seven-year recovery plan for the Kirtland's warbler in its only-known breeding area in Michigan is nearing final planning stages, and involves expanding potential habitat – young stands of jack pines – to accommodate an optimum number of 1,000 nesting birds. Here, controlled burning, timber harvesting and planting schemes will produce exactly the habitat that the bird requires.

In the words of Kai Curry-Lindahl, of the Survival Service Commission, "This is truly a remarkable instance of a government's capacity for humane action. It gives one hope for the future of wildlife when the mightiest nation in the world does so much to preserve a tiny bird."

EPILOGUE

In an age when many scientists are concerned about vanishing species, it is extraordinary for new animal species to continue to make themselves known at this late stage. Nevertheless, new mammals and birds continue to be discovered, while others are being rediscovered after all hope of their continued existence had long been exhausted.

On August 8, 1975, the National Geographic Society announced that an expedition to Paraguay's Chaco National Park in South America had discovered a brown, bristly-haired peccary with a long snout, thought to have long been extinct. In fact, the Chacoan peccary was previously known to science only as a fossil, dating back to the Pleistocene Age. Biology Professor Ralph Wetzel of the University of Connecticut, who made the find, said Indian hunters prized the "rangy, big pig" for its meat and hide. Until this discovery, only the collared and the white-lipped peccaries were known to have survived to the present. Also, in 1976 a subspecies of vole known as the Amargosa meadow vole *Microtis californicus scirpensis* was rediscovered in a desert area near Barstow, California, after having been thought extinct since 1917.

The start of 1977 brought to light another mammalian

discovery. A member of the marsupial family "Dasyuridae," new to science at that time, had been discovered in Billiatt Conservation Park, some 200 kilometres east of Adelaide in South Australia. It most closely resembles the genus *Antechinus*, but appears to merit a generic status itself; it has not yet been given a name. Dasyurids comprise most of Australia's small insectivorous and carnivorous marsupials, including the marsupial counterparts of the shrew.

A flower-eating bird believed extinct for a century was discovered in Peru in 1977. The bird was the white-winged guan, a bird slightly larger than a pheasant, weighing between two and a half and four and a half pounds, and measuring a little over three feet, including its tail. John O'Neill, a Louisiana State University ornithologist, and Gustavo del Solar of Peru, reported seeing four white-winged guans feeding in trees in the northwest part of the country on September 13, 1977. The discovery marked the first confirmed sighting of this species since 1877. In all, seventeen new bird species have been discovered in Peru since 1971, six discoveries of which can be attributed to John O'Neill. One reason for Peru's bonanza of birds is that the mountain country has not yet been studied thoroughly. "Moreover," says O'Neill, "the climate in the Andes has changed over the ages, leaving remote pockets of birds. Speciation, the evolutionary process which produces deviations in isolated groups, has yielded many new relatively isolated varieties." Peru, where O'Neill works, has more bird species than anywhere else except Colombia.

Despite the encouraging aspects of finding new species, and the rediscovering of supposed extinct species, plus the recovery of some endangered species, as earlier mentioned in this book, the number of species in peril continues to grow. Species such as the ivory-billed woodpecker *Campephilus principalis principalis*, Eskimo curlew *Numenius borealis* and the black-footed ferret *Mustela nigripes* are almost certain to become extinct, if in fact they are not already.

The current roster of vanishing animals on this continent is an awesome one. The following list of 162 species and subspecies all appear on the U.S. Department of the Interior, Fish and Wildlife

Service's federal register of endangered species in North America – as of July 14, 1977.

MAMMALS

Gray bat	*Myotis grisescens*
Hawaiian hoary bat	*Lasiurus cinereus semotus*
Indiana bat	*Myotis sodalis*
Wood bison	*Bison bison athabascae*
Eastern cougar	*Felis concolor cougar*
Columbian white-tailed deer	*Odocoileus virginianus leucurus*
Key deer	*Odocoileus virginianus clavium*
Black-footed ferret	*Mustela nigripes*
Northern kit fox	*Vulpes velox hebes*
San Joaquin kit fox	*Vulpes macrotis mutica*
Florida manatee	*Trichechus manatus latirostris*
Salt marsh harvest mouse	*Reithrodentomys raviventris*
Florida panther	*Felis concolor coryi*
Utah prairie dog	*Cynomys parvidens*
Peninsula pronghorn	*Antilocapra americana peninsularis*
Sonoran pronghorn	*Antilocapra americana sonoriensis*
Morro Bay kangaroo rat	*Dipodomys heermanni morroensis*
Delmarva peninsula fox squirrel	*Sciurus niger cinereus*
Hawaiian monk seal	*Monachus schauinslandi*
Eastern timber wolf	*Canis lupus lycaon*
Gray wolf	*Canis lupus monstrabilis*
Mexican wolf	*Canis lupus baileyi*
Northern Rocky Mountain wolf	*Canis lupus irremotus*
Red wolf	*Canis rufus*
Blue whale*	*Balaenoptera musculus*
Bowhead whale*	*Baleana mysticetus*
Finback whale*	*Balaenoptera physalus*
Gray whale*	*Eschrichtius gibbonsus*
Humpback whale*	*Megaptera novaeangliae*
Right whale*	*Eubaleana spp* (all species)
Sei whale*	*Balaenoptera borealis*
Sperm whale*	*Physter catodon*

* Listed as endangered on the United States World List.

BIRDS

Hawaii akepa	*Loxops coccinea coccinea*
Maui akepa	*Loxops coccinea ochracea*
Kauai akialoa	*Hemignathus procerus*
Akiapolaau	*Hemignathus wilsoni*
Masked bobwhite	*Colinus virginianus ridgwayi*
California condor	*Gymnogyps californianus*
Hawaiian coot	*Fulica americana alai*
Mississippi sandhill crane	*Grus canadensis pulla*
Whooping crane	*Grus americana*
Hawaii creeper	*Loxops maculata mana*
Molokai creeper	*Loxops maculata flammea*
Yellow-shouldered blackbird	*Agelaius xanthomus*
Oahu creeper	*Loxops maculata maculata*
Hawaiian crow	*Corvus tropicus*
Eskimo curlew	*Numenius borealis*
Palau ground dove	*Gallicolumba canifrons*
Hawaiian duck	*Anas wyvilliana*
Laysan duck	*Anas laysanensis*
Southern bald eagle	*Haliaeetus leucocephalus leucocephalus*
American peregrine falcon	*Falco peregrinus anatum*
Arctic peregrine falcon	*Falcon peregrinus tundrius*
Laysan finches and nihoa	*Psittirostra cantans*
Palau fantail flycatcher	*Rhipidura lepida*
Hawaiian gallinule	*Gallinula chloropus sandvicensis*
Aleutian Canada goose	*Branta canadensis leucopareia*
Hawaiian goose (nene)	*Branta sandvicensis*
Hawaiian hawk	*Buteo solitarius*
Crested honeycreeper	*Palmeria dolei*
Everglade kite	*Rostrhamus sociabilis plumbeus*
La Perouse's megapode	*Megapodius laperouse*
Nihoa millerbird	*Acrocephalus kingi*
Tinian monarch	*Monarcha takatsukasae*
Kauai & Maui nukupuus	*Hemignathus lucidus*
Kauai oo	*Moho braceatus*
Palau owl	*Otus podargina*
Palila	*Psittirostra bailloui*
Ou	*Psittirostra psittacea*
Puerto Rican parrot	*Amazona vittata*
Thick-billed parrot	*Rhynochopsitta pachyrhyncha*
Maui parrotbill	*Pseudonestor xanthophrys*
Brown pelican	*Pelecanus occidentalis*
Hawaiian dark-rumped petrel	*Pterodroma phaepygia sandwichensis*

Puerto Rican plain pigeon	*Columba palumbus azorica*
Poo-uli	*Melamprosops phaeosoma*
Attwater's greater prairie chicken	*Tympanuchus cupido attwateri*
California clapper rail	*Rallus longirostris obsoletus*
Light-footed clapper rail	*Rallus longirostris levipes*
Yuma clapper rail	*Rallus longirostris yumanensis*
Dusky seaside sparrow	*Ammospiza maritima nigrescens*
Cape Sable sparrow	*Ammospiza maritima mirabilis*
Santa Barbara song sparrow	*Meolspiza melodia graminea*
Ponape mountain starling	*Aplonis pelzelni*
Hawaiian stilt	*Himantopus himantopus knudseni*
California least tern	*Sterna albifrons browni*
Large Kauai thrush	*Phaeornis obscurus myadestina*
Molokai thrush	*Phaeornis obscurus rutha*
Small Kauai thrush	*Phaeornis palmeri*
Bachman's warbler	*Vermivora bachmanii*
Kirtland's warbler	*Dendroica kirtlandii*
Puerto Rican whip-poor-will	*Caprimulgus noctitherus*
Great Ponape white-eye	*Rukia sanfordi*
Ivory-billed woodpecker	*Campephilus principalis principalis*
Red-cockaded woodpecker	*Dendrocopos borealis*

REPTILES & AMPHIBIANS

Puerto Rican boa	*Epicrates inornatus*
American crocodile	*Crocodylus acutus*
Blunt-nose leopard lizard	*Crotaphytus silus*
San Francisco garter snake	*Thamnophis sirtalis tetrataenia*
Slender desert salamander	*Batrachoseps aridus*
Santa Cruz long-toed salamander	*Ambystoma macrodactylum croceum*
Texas blind salamander	*Typhlomolge rathbuni*
Houston toad	*Bufo houstonensis*

FISH

Pahranagat bonytail	*Gila robusta jordoni*
Humpback chub	*Gila cypha*
Mohave chub	*Gila (Siphateles) mohavensis*
Longjaw cisco	*Coregonus alpenae*
Cui-ui	*Chasmistes cujus*
Kendall Warm Springs dace	*Rhinichthys osculus thermalis*
Moapa dace	*Moapa coriacea*
Fountain darter	*Etheostoma fonticola*
Maryland darter	*Etheostoma sellare*

Okaloosa darter	*Etheostoma okaloosae*
Snail darter	*Percina tanasi*
Watercress darter	*Etheostoma nuchale*
Big Bend gambusia	*Gambusia gaigei*
Clear Creek gambusia	*Gambusia heterochir*
Pecos gambusia	*Gambusia nobilis*
Pahrump killifish	*Empetrichythys latos*
Scioto madtom	*Noturus trautmani*
Blue pike (walleye)	*Stizostedion vitreum glaucum*
Comanche Springs pupfish	*Cyprinodon elegans*
Devil's Hole pupfish	*Cyprinodon diabolis*
Owens River pupfish	*Cyprinodon radiosus*
Tecopa pupfish	*Cyprinodon nevadensis calidae*
Warm Springs pupfish	*Cyprinodon nevadensis pectoralis*
Colorado River squawfish	*Ptychocheilus lucius*
Unarmored three-spine stickleback	*Gasterosterus aculeatus williamsoni*
Shortnose sturgeon	*Acipenser brevirostrum*
Gila topminnow	*Poeciliopsis occidentalis*
Gila trout	*Salmo gilae*
Greenback cutthroat trout	*Salmo clarki stomias*
Woundfin	*Plagopterus argentissimus*

CLAMS

Alabama lamp pearly mussel	*Lampsilis virescens*
Appalachian monkeyface pearly mussel	*Quadrula sparsa*
Birdwing pearly mussel	*Conradilla caelata*
Cumberland bean pearly mussel	*Villosa trabilis*
Cumberland monkeyface pearly mussel	*Quadrula intermedia*
Curtis' pearly mussel	*Epioblasma florentina curtisi*
Dromedary pearly mussel	*Dromus dromas*
Fat pocketbook pearly mussel	*Potamilus capax*
Fine-rayed pigtoe pearly mussel	*Fusconaia cuncolus*
Green-blossom pearly mussel	*Epioblasma torulosa gubernaculum*
Higgin's eye pearly mussel	*Lampsilis higginsi*
Pale lilliput pearly mussel	*Toxolasma cylindrella*
Pink musket pearly mussel	*Lampsilis orbiculata orbiculata*
Rough pigtoe pearly mussel	*Pleurobema plenum*
Sampson's pearly mussel	*Epioblasma sampsoni*
Shiny pigtoe pearly mussel	*Fusconaia edgariana*
Tuberculed-blossom pearly mussel	*Epioblasma torulosa torulosa*
Turgid-blossom pearly mussel	*Epioblasma turgidula*

White cat's mussel	*Epioblasma sulcata delicata*
White warty-back pearly mussel	*Plethobasis cicattricosus*
Yellow-blossom pearly mussel	*Epioblasma florentina florentina*
Orange footed pimpleback	*Plethobasis cooperianus*

INSECTS

El Segundo blue butterfly	*Shijimiaeoides battoides allyni*
Lange's metalmark butterfly	*Apodemia mormo langei*
Lotis blue butterfly	*Lycaeides argyrognomon lotis*
Mission blue butterfly	*Icaricia icarioides missionensis*
San Bruno elfin butterfly	*Callophrys mossii bayensis*
Smith's blue butterfly	*Shijimiaeoides enoptes smithi*

The following eleven species have been designated as threatened species.

Grizzly bear	*Ursus arctos horribilis*
Southern sea otter	*Enhydra lutris nereis*
Newell's Manx shearwater	*Puffinus puffinus newelli*
American alligator	*Alligator mississippiensis*
Red Hills salamander	*Phaeognathus hubrichti*
Bayou darter	*Etheostoma rubrum*
Arizona trout	*Salmo apache*
Lahontan cutthroat trout	*Salmo clarki henshawi*
Paiute cutthroat trout	*Salmo clarki seleniris*
Bahama swallowtail butterfly	*Papilio andraemon bonhotei*
Schaus' swallowtail butterfly	*Papilio aristodemus ponceanus*

Despite a growing sense of conscience and the eagerness of many people both in and out of the scientific community to do something to save our dwindling wildlife, the question "What importance does the existence of a few wild animals have?" reflects the attitude of certain sections of the public. There is no use appealing to these people on esoteric grounds, pointing out simply that wild animals need to exist simply because they do exist. Wild creatures have been our neighbours on this planet for two million years and pre-date our relatively late arrival. They are part of the fabric of our lives.

History is replete with examples of evolution and change,

which are matters of considerable importance to man as an insight into his own future. Endangered species are barometers of the changes that are constantly occurring, that often go unnoticed, and the consequences of which are therefore difficult to ascertain. Man in all his wisdom does not yet have the experience to grasp the full significance of the loss of a single wildlife species as it may apply to himself. Human well-being is the total focus of all the aims, desires, and accomplishments that drive man on this planet.

A little more than a century ago a man could watch by the hour as millions of passenger pigeons winged overhead, literally shutting out the sun. A little more than half a century ago, the last passenger pigeon on earth died in a zoo without issue. A little more than a century ago one might have watched by the hour as a herd of bison thundered across the plains. A little more than half a century ago the American bison had been reduced to a few stragglers. But a spark of concern caught fire, and the bison was brought back from the edge of oblivion to continue as a part of our natural heritage. Other fortunate species were to follow.

Today, the future of many kinds of wildlife species depends on that continued concern. Aldo Leopold made an observation on the extinction of the passenger pigeon:

> For one species to mourn the death of another is a new thing under the sun. We, who have lost our pigeons, mourn the loss. Had the funeral been ours, the pigeons would hardly have mourned us. In this fact, rather than in nylons or atomic bombs, lies evidence of our superiority over the beasts.

Our superiority over wildlife species should carry with it an equal proportion of responsibility. This cannot now be ignored, for as can be seen in cases of the bison, the beaver, the trumpeter swan, the pronghorn, and other former vanishing species that flourish today, when our concern is strong enough we have the power to save imperilled wildlife.

BIBLIOGRAPHY

Allen, G.M. 1942. *Extinct and Vanishing Mammals of the Western Hemisphere.* Special Publication of American Comm. Int.

Allen, R. 1974. *Vanishing Wildlife of North America.* National Geographic Society.

Allen, R.P. *Whooping Crane Report.* Research Report No. 3. National Audubon Society.

Baker, J.A. 1967. *The Peregrine.* London: Collins.

Banfield, A. and N.S. Novakowski. 1960. *The Survival of the Wood Bison in the Northwest Territories.* National Museum of Canada.

Banko, W.E. 1960. *The Trumpeter Swan: its habit, history, and population in the United States.* North American Fauna, No. 63. U.S. Fish and Wildlife Service.

Bent, A.C. 1912. Notes of birds observed during a brief visit to the Aleutian Islands and Bering Sea in 1911. Smithsonian Institution, Miscellaneous Collection 56(32).

Boolootian, R.A. 1962. "California's Sea Otter." *Animals*: 3, 12.

Bruemmer, F. 1972. *Encounters with Arctic Animals.* Toronto: McGraw Hill/Ryerson Ltd.

Byrd, G.V. and P.F. Springer. 1976. Recovery Program for the Endangered Aleutian Canada Goose. California-Nevada Wildlife Transactions.

Cahalane, V.H. 1947. *Mammals of North America.* New York: The Macmillan Company.

Caras, R. 1966. *Last Chance on Earth.* New York: Clifton Books.

Cooley, R.A. 1968. International Scientific Cooperation on the Polar Bear. IUCN Bulletin: 54-56.

Curry-Lindahl, K. 1972. *Let Them Live.* New York: William Morrow and Company Inc.

Duke of Edinburgh, H.R.H. and J. Fisher. 1970. *Wildlife Crisis.* New York: Cowles Book Company Ltd.

Fisher, J., N. Simon and J. Vincent. 1969. *The Red Book-Wildlife in Danger.* (Popular narrative version of the IUCN's famous red data books.) London: Collins.

Fitter, R. 1968. *Vanishing Wild Animals of the World.* Published by the Midland Bank.

Fyfe, R. 1976. "Bringing Back the Peregrine Falcon." *Nature Canada,* vol. 5, no. 2.

Godfrey, W.E. 1966. *Birds of Canada.* National Museum of Canada. Ottawa.

Godfrey, W.E. 1970. "Rare or Endangered Canadian Birds." *Canadian Field Naturalist.* January-March, 1970.

Grossman, M.L. and S., and J. Hamlet. 1969. *Vanishing Wilderness.* New York: Madison Square Press.

Guggisberg, C.A.W. 1970. *Man and Wildlife.* New York: Arco Publishing Company.

Hagar, J.A. 1966. Nesting of the Hudsonian Godwit at Churchill, Manitoba. The Laboratory of Ornithology. Cornell University, Ed. 5.

Hall, G.H. 1955. *Great Moments in Action—The Story of the Sun Life Falcons.* Montreal: Mercury Press, 1-37.

Harrington, C.R. 1965. "The Life and Status of the Polar Bear." *Oryx* VIII, 3.

Hope, C.E. and T.M. Shortt. 1944. "Southward Migration of Adult Shorebirds on the West Coast of James Bay." *The Auk,* vol. 61.

International Union for the Conservation of Nature and Natural Resources (IUCN) Red Data Books, vols. I and II. Morges, Switzerland.

Jones, R.D. Jr. 1963. Buldir Island, Site of a Remnant Breeding Population of Aleutian Canada Geese. Annual Rep. Wildfowl Trust 14.

Koford, C.B. 1953. "The California Condor," National Audubon Society, Rep. no. 4.

Kolenosky, G. and R.O. Standfield. 1966. "Polar Bears of Canada." *Animals* 8(19): 528-531.

Kuyt, E. 1976. "Whooping Cranes–The Long Road Back." *Nature Canada*, vol. 5, no. 2.

Line, L. 1964. The Jack-Pine Warbler Story. Michigan Audubon Society. November-December.

MacCrimmon, H.R. 1977. *Animals, Man, and Change.* Toronto: McClelland and Stewart.

Mackenzie, J.P.S. and T.M. Shortt. 1977. *Birds in Peril.* Toronto: McGraw Hill/Ryerson Ltd.

MacMillan, I. 1968. *Man and California Condors.* New York: E.P. Dutton & Co.

Matthiessen, P. 1959. *Wildlife in America.* New York: The Viking Press.

Mayfield, H.F. 1960. The Kirtland's Warbler. Cranbrook Institute of Science. Michigan.

Mayfield, H.F. 1972. "Third Dicennial Census of Kirtland's Warbler." *The Auk*, vol. 89.

McNulty, F. 1966. *The Whooping Crane.* New York: E.P. Dutton & Company.

Milne, L. and M. Milne. 1971. *The Cougar Doesn't Live Here Anymore.* Englewood Cliffs, New Jersey: Prentice-Hall.

Mitchell, M.H. 1935. *The Passenger Pigeon in Ontario.* Toronto: University of Toronto Press.

Morrell, S.H. 1975. San Joaquin Kit Fox Distribution and Abundance in 1975. California Department of Fish and Game, Wildlife Management.

Murie, O.J. 1936. Biological Investigations, Aleutian Islands & Southwestern Alaska. U.S. Fish and Wildlife Service, April 23-Sept. 19.

Nero, R.W. 1973. *The Great White Bears*. Province of Manitoba, Department of Mines, Resources, and Environment Management.

Novakowski, N.S. 1970. "Rare or Endangered Canadian Mammals." *Canadian Field Naturalist*, January-March 1970.

Palmisano, Dr. A.W. "The Alligator: A Wildlife Resource in Louisiana," *Louisiana Conservationist*.

Perry, R. 1973. *The Polar Worlds*. New York: Taplinger Publishing Company.

Peterson, R.T. 1948. *Birds over America*. New York: Dodd Mead & Company.

Peterson, R.T. 1974. Proceedings of the Symposium of Endangered and Threatened Species of North America.

Pinney, Roy. 1966. *Wildlife in Danger*. New York: Duell, Sloan and Pearce.

Ruddy, J. and D. Stewart. 1971. "And Then There Were None." *Maclean's*. April, p. 1; May, p. 12.

Silverberg, R. 1967. *The Auk, The Dodo, and the Oryx*. New York: Thomas Crowell Co.

Simon, N. and P. Gerondet. 1970. *Last Survivors*. New York: The World Publ. Co.

Stewart, D. 1974. *Canadian Endangered Species*. New York: Gage Publishing.

Stewart, D. 1975. "Endangered Species." Federation of Ontario Naturalists, *Ontario Naturalist*, June.

Tener, J.S. 1967. Vanishing Species in Canada. Presented at the International Association of Fish, Game, and Conservation Commission, Toronto.

Tennesen, M. 1976. "Good Times: The Sea Otter." *National Wildlife*. Feb./March.

Tennesen, M. 1976. "Phantoms of the Prairie." *National Wildlife*, vol. 14, no. 4. June/July.

Ullrich, and Tylinek. 1971. *Endangered Species*. New York: Hart Publishing Co. Inc.

Vollmar, F. 1968. The Ark Under Way: Second Report of the World Wildlife Fund, 1965-1967. Lausanne.

Walden, F.A. 1973. Endangered Species in Ontario. Presented at the Annual Meeting of the Federation of Ontario Naturalists.

Wetmore, A. 1956. A check-list of the fossil and prehistoric birds of North America and the West Indies. Smithsonian Misc. Coll. 131 (5): 105 pp.

Wood, F. and D. Wood. 1968. *Animals in Danger.* New York: Dodd Mead & Co.

Wormer, J. Van. 1969. *The World of the Pronghorn.* Philadelphia: J.B. Lippincott Co.

Zimmerman, D.R. 1974. "Captive Breeding: Boon or Boondoggle." *Natural History,* December.